Image of the Jews

Teachers' Guide to
JEWS and their RELIGION

EUGENE BOROWITZ

IRVING GREENBERG

JULES HARLOW

MAX J. ROUTTENBERG

DORE SCHARY

MICHAEL WYSCHOGROD

Foreword by Brother Joseph Irwin, F.S.C.
Teachers' Guide by Ruth Seldin

ANTI-DEFAMATION LEAGUE OF B'NAI B'RITH

PUBLISHED FOR THE
ANTI-DEFAMATION LEAGUE OF B'NAI BRITH
BY
KTAV PUBLISHING HOUSE, INC.
NEW YORK, NEW YORK 10002

SBN 87068-014-5 .

Publication of this book was made possible by a generous gift
in memory of Aaron M. Becker

LIBRARY OF CONGRESS CATALOG CARD NUMBER: 74-114981
MANUFACTURED IN THE UNITED STATES OF AMERICA

FOREWORD

At the heart of any ecumenical endeavor must be the genuine acceptance of the other precisely as *other*. Adequate understanding necessarily precedes any quality-type acceptance. Yet few, if any, Catholic high-school teachers can speak of praiseworthy gains in presenting Judaism as such to their students. Thus, the present work answers a definite need.

In promoting this manual, the office of the Anti-Defamation League of B'nai B'rith is actually challenging the coming of age on the part of Catholic teachers in the sense that they present the *whole* of religion to their students. For one of the advantages of the ecumenical age, called for by the Fathers of Vatican II, is that Catholic people in general can now measure their mature security in Catholic belief by recognizing more fully the values of persons of other religions who profess abiding faith and belief. Paradoxically, it is those with the deepest beliefs who openly seek to comprehend the beliefs of others. Put another way, "If Christianity has something to give, it has also much to receive. It cannot fully be itself until it has encountered all people."*

In so many ways, it seems that theologically the twain shall not meet in the foreseeable future with regard to Jewish-Christian cooperation. At the center of things, it must seem a hard saying to Jews when Christians speak of believing in the same one true God, and yet believe in Him as a Trinity. Because of this and the liturgical reasons of language and ritual, cooperative Jewish-Christian worship does not hold much promise at the present time. Apart from moral emulation and joint social endeavor, the one thing left to the Christian, it seems, is to know in a personally-felt way how the Jew tends to see himself. And Catholic high-school teachers surely have a role to play here.

---

*Moran, Gabriel and Maria Harris. *Experiences in Community,* New York: Herder & Herder, 1968, p. 32.

Finally, Catholic religion teachers would do well to become personally involved with Jewish believers. Thanks to Mrs. Ruth Seldin and the staff at the Anti-Defamation League, I feel that my newly-found insights into Jews and Judaism are more personal than professional (although the latter have been supplied in abundance). The conviction that what Christians call the Old Testament is very much alive today in the persons of Jews the world over will be the force that motivates Catholic teachers to use this manual effectively.

BROTHER JOSEPH IRWIN, F.S.C.

TABLE OF CONTENTS

CONTRIBUTORS

DORE SCHARY
> Noted playwright and director; Honorary National Chairman of the Anti-Defamation League of B'nai B'rith.

RABBI IRVING GREENBERG
> Associate Professor of History, Yeshiva University; Rabbi of the Riverdale Jewish Center, Riverdale, New York.

RABBI EUGENE BOROWITZ
> Author and lecturer; Professor of Education and Jewish Religious Thought, Hebrew Union College-Jewish Institute of Religion, New York.

RABBI JULES HARLOW
> Director of publications of the Rabbinical Assembly of America; editor of a series of new liturgical publications published by the Rabbinical Assembly.

RABBI MAX J. ROUTTENBERG
> Rabbi, Temple B'nai Sholom, Rockville Center, N.Y.; former president of the Rabbinical Assembly of America, former executive vice-president and Visiting Professor of Homiletics, Jewish Theological Seminary of America.

DR. MICHAEL WYSCHOGROD
> Associate Professor of Philosophy, Baruch College, City University of New York; member of the editorial board of *Tradition* and of *Judaism*.

PREFACE

What follows is the first extensive body of instructional material on Judaism to be prepared especially for the Catholic high school. (The reader will note that this material can be easily used in Protestant schools as well.) The closed-circuit television (or filmed) programs that comprise this series and this teachers' guide—joint projects of the Archdiocese of New York, under the supervision of Msgr. John T. Doherty, then Associate Superintendent of Schools and Director of Religious Education, and now Executive Secretary for the Ecumenical and Liturgical Commissions, and the Anti-Defamation League of B'nai B'rith—are ground-breaking endeavors, pioneers in what must become an increasing flow of resources to aid in Christian-Jewish dialogue.

There is surely no disputing the need for such dialogue. Among Catholics as among Jews, the lack of knowledge of the others' religion, attitudes, life style and intentions is appalling. When this project was initiated, a teaching Brother at one of the Catholic high schools in New York City asked approximately 100 of his students to write down, briefly, what they knew about Jews and Judaism. A few of the comments displayed sensitive awareness, if not formal knowledge; a few betrayed outright anti-Semitism; the bulk showed good will—and no knowledge.

Assuming these responses to be fairly representative (and, incidentally, such an approach—i.e., asking the students what they know about a subject without any previous discussion or briefing—may be both useful and informative in any classroom situation), the prime purpose of this book is to help the individual Catholic teacher by providing a basic fund of information and by offering a systematic approach to the study of the Jewish religion. Attitudes, prejudices, stereotypes, biases—these are not easily dealt with. Teachers always hope that increased knowledge will help to dissipate prejudices, and in this respect the guide—especially the suggested discussion topics and classroom activities—should prove useful. However, no guide can possibly deal with all facets of student attitudes, and so answers to many questions that will arise will have to be sought elsewhere.

A special word of thanks is due ADL staff for their conscientious, skillful and creative teamwork in bringing this project to fulfillment; to Ruth Seldin for accomplishing the difficult task of organizing a mass of detail and making it into a clear and stimulating teachers' guide; and to her consultant on this work, Brother Joseph Irwin, F.S.C., of Cardinal Spellman High School for his thoughtful suggestions and advice. Mrs Seldin's and Brother Joseph's commitment and dedication to this project made their collaboration a small miracle of interreligious cooperation.

It is hoped, needless to say, that this guide and the series of filmed lectures will be used and used well, and that a study of the Jews and their religion will prove enriching for teacher and student alike. Above all, it is hoped that this study of Jews and Judaism will lead to greater harmony, better understanding and improved relations between members of the two faiths.

BENJAMIN R. EPSTEIN,
NATIONAL DIRECTOR,
ANTI-DEFAMATION LEAGUE
OF B'NAI B'RITH

WHO IS THE AMERICAN JEW?

Dore Schary

Introduction: Definition of the American Jew

The simplest questions often give us the greatest difficulty.

The Jew has been on the stage' of history for a long time. He has lived everywhere and has shared in many of the great moments which have directed the course of human destiny. Some say that more has been written about the Jewish people than any other people; and surely the word Jew is one of the most used and abused in the dictionary of mankind. Yet until now nobody has really succeeded in giving us a clear-cut answer to the question, "Who is a Jew?"

The Jew is as perplexed about a proper definition of himself as is the non-Jew. No less a source than the government of the State of Israel set up a special committee in 1958 to inquire of leading Jewish scholars throughout the world: Who is a Jew? The results, while interesting enough, were inconclusive.

Though, on the face of it, my task is more limited—after all, I shall only be discussing the question "Who are the *American* Jews"?—what I shall have to say will not, I suspect, provide the definitive answer either. It may, as a matter of fact, raise still other questions and challenge some of our most firmly-held concepts. It will, I hope, stimulate us into hard and serious thinking. And who knows?—perhaps one of you will be so inspired that he or she will at long last provide us with an answer which will satisfy everyone.

Jewish Identity

Before plunging into this absorbing topic, I think it might be interesting to cite at least one man's view on the subject. I have in mind the late Rabbi Morris Adler, one of the leaders in American Conservative Judaism. This is what he had to offer:

Based on the original script delivered on closed-circuit television.

1

The modern Jew is not only a riddle unto himself. He senses that he is likewise a mystery to his Gentile neighbors, even though many myths touching the Jew have been dissolved in our time. The Jew no longer dwells behind ghetto walls. He shares the culture, the mores, the preoccupations and diversions of his non-Jewish neighbors, who are often his friends. Yet there remains something enigmatic in his relationship with Gentiles.

I recall, for example, my own experience when I was an Army Chaplain during World War II. I was on most cordial terms with the other Chaplains, both Catholic and Protestant. We shared the same tents, jumped into the same foxholes. Our dislike of certain of our superiors was also shared. We thus had much in common. Perhaps because it was contrary to Army regulations I decided one day to grow a beard. The consequences were surprising. My beard seemed to add a new dimension to my relationship with my fellow Chaplains. I think this was because my identity had suddenly become clearer and more intelligible. After all, the last Jew they really knew about was Jesus, who is always pictured with a beard. Clean-shaven like the rest, wearing a uniform, I provided no continuity with this Jewish image of theirs. I bore the designation Jew, yet they were perplexed as to what kind of a being I really was. My beard changed matters; I was now no great mystery.

The American Jew thinks of himself as a doctor, a businessman, a worker, a citizen, a father—just like other Americans. Then he discovers a puzzlement in the eyes of his neighbors—and the question mark quickly moves into his own mind. So he comes home and asks: "Who after all am I?"

Perhaps the best way to reach at least the beginnings of an answer to the question of Jewish identity is to take a look at the present-day American Jewish community and see how it evolved. Composed of almost six million people, which makes it the largest concentration of Jews within one land in world history, the Jewish community in the United States is largely a middle-class one—well educated, mobile, active in numerous organizations and movements. Though it has no central authority, no one framework of reference, and no one delineated sphere of action, it is held together by a feeling of group interdependence and a common spiritual and cultural heritage. At the same time, it is a community built up as much by social change and external needs as by any preconceived or internal planning.

American Jews today are not only the largest but the most influential Jewish community anywhere. However, they did not really assume this role until the rise of Hitler and the subsequent slaughter of some six million European Jews. During this dark moment in human history, the Jews in this country were instrumental in organizing a mighty effort to rescue those Jews who still survived, as well as to shore up their refuge, Israel.

Yet, though it is true that Israel is now a state, fulfilling thus the ancient dream and belief that the Jewish people would one day reestablish their nation in Palestine, only a handful of American Jews have felt the wish to live there. Jews in America were stirred, of course, by the rebirth of Israel; have been deeply concerned for its safety and survival, particularly during the recent Six-Day War. And, perhaps most important of all, to many it has given a deeper appreciation of their Jewish identity. But Jews here have not simply lived through too much, they have given and received too much to be anything but Americans, or to view this country as anything but their home.

Nothing could be more natural, after all; for, after generations of restrictions in Europe's ghettos, the opportunity to become a significant part of the prevailing secular culture was heady wine, indeed. And with the passionate struggle for self-improvement that was born of this opportunity came a source of new pride. As a consequence, the conflict that once existed for many American Jews— *i.e.,* between practicing Judaism, and participating in the mainstream of American life—has become more and more muted, and a unique pattern of Jewish life is increasingly developing in the United States. It is a pattern that unites 5,000 years of tradition with 300 years of growth and experience in a free land.

Earliest History of the American Jewish Community (1654-63)

Let us take, then, a glance at the history of these 300 years. The first Jewish settlement in what is now the United States took place as far back as September 1654, with the arrival of 23 Portuguese Jews in New Amsterdam. In less than ten years, they won from Governor Peter Stuyvesant not just the right to buy real estate and engage in retail trade, but to bear arms and join the militia in defense of their new homeland. Likewise their right to worship at home was respected.

Jewish Immigration From Europe (1800-80)

Within a short time other Jews, most of whom came from central Europe, settled elsewhere in the 13 colonies. This early wave of Jewish immigration was quite small, however. By 1800 there were all told not more than 2,500 Jews scattered through the United States, and only six congregations had built synagogues.

In the sixty years from 1820 to 1880, a second and far larger wave of Jewish immigrants, most of them from Germany and the Austro-Hungarian Empire, hit the American shores. These Jews were to play an important role in the expansion westward of the United States. Many of them put peddlers' packs on their backs and headed for new frontiers. They helped open the lands that were to become West Virginia, Ohio, Kentucky, Indiana, Illinois and Missouri; carried supplies to Indians, trappers and farmers; built paper and hemp mills.

When a Jewish peddler accumulated enough capital to open a store at a crossroads, he settled down. As a result, you can drive across America today, and eat and sleep in towns named after their pioneering Jewish founders—from Gilman, Connecticut and Aaronsburg, Pennsylvania to Roseville, California and Heppner, Oregon.

Thousands of Jews, in the North and South, fought and served in the American Civil War. After the war was over, Jews continued to move westward, sinking their roots deep into such frontier cities as St. Louis, Cincinnati and San Francisco. They entered into all aspects of industry and commerce, and their efforts contributed in no small measure to the industrial growth of our nation.

A New Life in America (1882-1920's)

The third and largest wave of Jewish immigration, this time from Eastern Europe, began in 1882 and continued until the restrictive immigration laws of the early 1920's cut it to a trickle. Under the lash of pogroms in Russia, restrictions in Roumania and poverty in Austria-Hungary, almost two million Jews sought a new life in the United States. They were almost entirely Yiddish-speaking. They were desperately poor, reaching America with an average of nine dollars. The majority of them found employment in the garment industry in New York City, and lived on the Lower East Side which at its peak housed over one-and-a-half million Jews.

To give you some flavor of what life was like for these immigrants on their arrival in this country, let us turn for an instant to a typical letter— of which there were many—addressed by one such immigrant to the Yiddish paper, *The Forward:*

March 6, 1906

Dear Mr. Editor:

I am a greenhorn. I have only been five weeks in the country. I am
a jewelry maker. I left a blind father and a stepmother in Russia.
Before my departure my father begged me not to forget him. I
promised that I would send him the first money I should earn.
I walked around two weeks and looked for work. But at the end
of the third week I succeeded in getting a job. I worked a week and
received eight dollars for the week. I paid for my board and bought
certain necessities, such as a hat, shoes, and some small items, and
I have a few dollars, too. Now, Mr. Editor, I want to ask you to
give me some advice as to what to do. Should I send my father
a few dollars for Passover, or should I keep them for myself?
Because the work at our place is at end, and I may have to be without work. So that I do not know what to do. I hope you will give
me some advice in my difficulties, and I shall obey you just as you
tell me.

Y. Mednikoff

There is enough evidence to warrant the observation that these immigrant Jews had by the turn of the century become the most industrialized
ethnic group in the City of New York. This began to change, however,
as they increasingly responded to the occupational needs and economic
demands of the twentieth century by directing their vocational aspirations, and in particular those of their children, towards the professions
and white-collar occupations. To achieve this step up the ladder, education was obviously necessary.

Secular Education and Its Results

Education had always had deep roots in Jewish consciousness, representing not only an ideal to strive for but a religious duty and a way of
life. In fact, there is an old Jewish saying that a father "will bend the
sky" to give his sons the best education possible. In Biblical times the
instruction of children in *Torah,* or the Jewish law, was regarded as the
solemn duty of all parents. During the Middle Ages, schools that gave
education to boys were as important to each and every Jewish community as the synagogue itself. For how could one hope to communicate
with God if one had not studied and could not read and understand the
words of the prayers and the Bible?

Our modern world, too, has witnessed this continued emphasis by
Jews on education. With one major change. From an emphasis on re-

ligious training, the majority of Eastern European Jewish immigrants shifted to a more secular approach in their struggle for self-improvement and integration within the American community at large. Thus, while many of them lived in cold-water tenements, they nonetheless saw to it that their sons were sent to college and to professional schools.

The results of this educational effort have been impressive, to say the least. By 1916, the Jewish population on New York's lower East Side had shrunk to only 350,000 and by 1930, to 100,000, reflecting the mobility of an educated people. The same was true of Chicago, where the ghetto area lost half its Jews between 1914 and 1920. Everywhere, in fact, Jews improved their occupational and residential status.

The figures in the field of education are equally arresting. A contemporary study has revealed that there are more than 300,000 Jewish students enrolled in American school of higher education, and that there is a similarly large proportion of Jews in the academic community. At the same time, surveys of Jewish education in New York City taken within the last ten years show that, of all students over 18 who had completed college, there were almost four times as many Jews as non-Jews. In smaller communities, the proportion is believed to be even higher.

For the past several decades, Jews have been extremely active in all the professions, arts and sciences, and have had a profound effect on American life. In law, one can cite Benjamin Cardozo, Louis Brandeis, Felix Frankfurter; in medicine, Selman Waksman and Jonas Salk; in physics, Albert Einstein and Isidore Rabi; in the arts, Leonard Bernstein, Arthur Miller, George Gershwin, and Herman Wouk; in government, Herbert H. Lehman, Anna Rosenberg and Jacob Javits. And these are only a few names picked at random from a very lengthy list.

Discrimination and the Fight Against It

As Jews entered increasingly into the main currents of American life, this trend was accompanied by the outbreak of considerable antagonism and discrimination. For the first time in American history, socially-based anti-Semitism appeared, and anti-Jewish exclusion started to spread through white Protestant society: its clubs, hotels and residential districts. More important still, by the early 1920's, in colleges, professional schools and at the managerial and executive level of many large corporations, quota systems were imposed against Jews which have begun to disappear only in recent years.

To combat the various forms of anti-Jewish discrimination, a number of organizations were created within the Jewish community. In 1906, the American Jewish Committee was formed, with the prime purpose of dealing with discrimination in business and industry. In 1913, the Anti-Defamation League, the civil rights and educational arm of B'nai B'rith, was set up to achieve better understanding between individuals and groups that compose the ethnic, religious and racial fabric of this nation. Lastly, in 1917, the American Jewish Congress was organized, representing the aspirations and ideals of many of the newest East European immigrants. Today, all three of these human relations agencies are energetic champions of civil rights; and, though they sometimes employ different means to achieve their commonly-held objectives, their concern for human betterment has never lost its ancient Jewish roots.

Jewish Philanthropy and Welfare

Jews have also had a long tradition in the American labor movement. Samuel Gompers founded the American Federation of Labor and was its president for 37 years. Sidney Hillman, late head of the CIO Political Action Committee, and David Dubinsky, president of the International Ladies' Garment Workers Union, were likewise products of Jewish unions which arose in protest against the low pay and long hours in the old "sweatshops."

The traditional Jewish concern for human betterment found even greater expression in the less tumultuous area of philanthropy. If any one impulse can be said to be commonly characteristic of Jews, it is devotion to charity. This impulse is deeply grounded in ancient religious tradition, which placed the highest premium on charity and lovingkindness in the hierarchy of values that make up the Jewish way of life. It is well illustrated by the following quotation from the Midrash, a collection of commentaries on the biblical text:

> In the future world, a man will be asked, 'What was your occupation?' If he reply, 'I fed the hungry,' then the reply is, 'This is the gate of the Lord; he who feeds the hungry, let him enter.'

> So too with giving drink to the thirsty, clothing the naked, sheltering the homeless, with those who look after orphans, and with those generally who do deeds of lovingkindness. All these are gates of the Lord, and those who do such deeds shall enter within them.

The catalogue of American Jewish welfare is endless. The American Red Cross was organized in Washington, D.C., home of Adolfus S. Solomons. Julius Rosenwald of Chicago established a $30-million fund for Negro welfare and education as part of his lifetime contribution of $70 million to charity. The three Strauss brothers of New York, Isadore, Nathan and Oscar were almost as generous. They built hospitals and tuberculosis sanitariums, set up relief stations that dispensed more than a million meals during the depression winter of 1914-15, led the fight for the pasteurization of New York City's milk supply and helped build a Roman Catholic Church. And then there is the Guggenheim family, of course, who set up a foundation, which since 1925 has given educational fellowships to thousands of artists, writers, scholars and scientists.

Hundreds of institutions for human welfare scattered over the nation are Jewish in creation and Jewish in support, although the bulk of the beneficiaries are non-Jewish. In its early days the Henry Street Settlement in New York, which was founded by Lillian D. Wald and financed by Jacob H. Schiff, became a world model for creative social work and was the cradle of the visiting nurse service.

Another Jewish innovation is the Council of Jewish Federations and Welfare Funds, an association of community organizations which coordinates the many national and international appeals (such as the energetic United Jewish Appeal for overseas aid) and analyzes the needs and finances of each.

Jewish women have been especially vigorous in welfare and civic work. Hadassah, one of the most influential women's organizations, is particularly active in Israel. Another leading group, the B'nai B'rith women, with chapters throughout the United States, is busily engaged in civic, charitable and humanitarian affairs, and works closely in coordination with the ADL in the area of civil rights.

The Jewish Home

I would like to say a few words at this point about another aspect of American Jewish life which has long served as perhaps the major reinforcement of Jewish social consciousness and tradition, in other words, the home, the family.

Any attempt to sketch a rough sociological picture of the contemporary American Jewish family as distinct from other American family groups must begin by acknowledging the fact that the sweeping social and economic changes of our times have affected all American families. Such developments as the increasing number of working wives and mothers and the vast movement to the suburbs, to name just two, have cut across group lines. However, certain customs, associations and values have helped the Jewish family withstand many of the disruptive influences of modern life by preserving itself against some of the disorganization that is currently widespread in American family life. It likewise maintains a definite Jewishness through the home-centered observance of festivals and holy days, although the formal ritual content of many of these ceremonies has changed considerably in recent years. Education is a prime value, and the family retains an undiminished sense of loyalty and cohesiveness.

The Synagogue and Religious Education

Just as Jewish life on the individual level centers in the home, so within the community it revolves around the synagogue. This is particularly true of suburbia. In almost every suburb where there are a hundred or more Jewish families, a new synagogue is rising. Though many of the members have had little or no contact with synagogues since childhood, they want their children to be introduced and made aware of their Jewish heritage and the Hebrew language. As a consequence, synagogue membership has increased in the past 20 years from about a third of the Jewish population to well over one-half. This upsurge has been felt by all three major Jewish groups, the Orthodox, the Conservative and the Reform. In addition to the traditional role as a place of worship, the synagogue of today—like the Jewish community center—has developed into a central meeting place for a number of activities which express the way of life of the Jew in America.

The American Jew of Today

The moment has come, I think, when we can look back at the foregoing discussion and attempt, if not a definition, at least a tentative description of who and what is the American Jew. Certainly one thing that emerges is that, to the American Jew, Judaism is not only a religion, but something very much more—a whole way of life, in fact. A way of life which has evolved through history and tradition and which includes literature and language, music and art, ethics and law. Thus, the secular as well as the religious Jew can feel at home within the many aspects of American Jewish culture.

The American Jew, though he identifies fully with the land of his birth, is at the same time part and parcel of the Jewish people. For this reason, he can—for all his Americanness—identify with the suffering of the Russian Jew, be proud of the achievements of the Israeli Jew. This bond that unites Jewry throughout the world is ever-present and, while at times it appears to be obscured, it invariably rises to the surface during some crisis situation.

Israel

Perhaps the clearest example of what I have just said can be seen with regard to Israel. Israel occupies a position in the minds and hearts of Jews in America that is unique. Unlike the Irish Catholics, for example, who with the passage of time and the process of acculturization, are tied today to their original homelands by gossamer strings, the American Jews have a different relationship with the nation of Israel. The bond which has always existed between the people of Israel and the Land of Israel is one that is unbreakable to the modern Jew, regardless of where he lives. American Jews hold their heads higher because of the existence and the achievements of Israel. Similarly, American Jewish concern for Israel remains as steadfast and as strong as ever and, as was seen during the Six Day War of June 1967, it can rise to a tremendous pitch of emotional fervor.

It is true, of course, that the position and attitude of American Jews to Israel can differ—even significantly, sometimes. Many still envision it as the fountainhead of Jewish culture and religion which ensures the continuance of many highly prized Jewish values and from which they can draw a powerful sense of identity. Others are less ardent, less emotionally involved. They wish Israel well, but expect it to develop a national existence largely independent of American-Jewish relations. But no American Jew is indifferent to, detached from, or unaware of the modern State of Israel.

Summary and Conclusions

In any case, and no matter what his ultimate attitude, the American Jew is a full-time resident and a full-time achiever in his native land, even while he aids and contributes to his Jewish brothers throughout the world. In fact, in ennobling and enhancing his own Jewish culture, he at the same time enriches the American scene in which he moves and draws breath. The freedom he has found under American democracy has thus been a blessing of opportunity and of achievement for himself as well as for all Americans.

Thus, American Judaism today is robust and looks to the future with confidence. It is generating spiritual and creative energy from which all people will benefit. Its good health is one sure proof that America's concept of equality under the law works. From New Amsterdam to the new suburbia, the Jews have struggled to make one of the most ancient religious cultures part of the growth of an ever-evolving and nobler America. They have contributed to America; they have grown with America. And, while their faith is still being tested here, it is being tested not by restriction, but by freedom—not by failure, but by success.

WHAT IS JUDAISM?

Rabbi Irving Greenberg

Introduction: What is Judaism?

"Without your permission you are born, without your permission you die," say the rabbis. How you live, however, is an act of choice. Judaism believes that all of life is, or can be, holy. To be holy is to be special: in a special relationship to God, to act in special ways to one's fellow man, to be oneself in a special way. Today I would like to examine how Judaism came to believe this, and how, and in what special ways, it teaches men to live. In short, what is Judaism, what does Judaism mean, and what are the values and acts by which Jews and ultimately all mankind should live?

Affirmations of Judaism

Judaism affirms that man is a person of infinite worth; that he is the object of God's love; and that, irrespective of his race, color or creed, he is created in the image of God. Judaism also affirms that all mankind will ultimately be redeemed because man is meant to be free and to live in dignity and peace. Judaism affords the Jews a way of life based on these affirmations and designed to bring about their fulfillment.

Jews know that these affirmations are true not just through reason, but through certain acts of God in human history. Judaism began when God called Abraham: "For I have known him, (*i.e.*, communicated with him) to the end that he may command his children and his household after him, that they may keep the way of the Lord, to do righteousness and justice . . ." (Genesis 18, 19).

Based on the original script delivered on closed-circuit television.

The Bible and the Covenant

The Bible teaches that Abraham was chosen not only for his unusual qualities as a human being, but because of the mystery of God's love for man. However, the choice of Abraham was not an exclusive one, meant to give special privilege to his seed. Rather ". . . in thee (through thee)," says the Bible, "shall all the families of the earth be blessed" (Genesis 12, 3).

This covenant that God made with Abraham he also made with his descendants, the people of Israel. Through the Exodus and the redemption of Israel from slavery to freedom, God placed his seal on the covenant he had already made with Abraham. In a world of oppression, poverty and the easy destruction of human life, the Exodus taught the Jew that God regarded man as the most precious of all His creatures, and as the object of His love. Judaism involves, then, the living out of this understanding of God's purpose in the life of the individual, in his interpersonal relationships and in society. This event and its symbolic meaning is the star by which the Jew walks through life and through history.

The Exodus

The Exodus and, by implication, its symbolic meaning and broad applicability to everyday life, are central threads of the biblical word. Thus, on the question of social ethics, the Torah says: "If a stranger (really, the outsider) sojourn with thee in your land, ye shall not do him wrong. The stranger that sojourneth with you shall be unto you as the home-born among you, and thou shalt love him as thyself; for ye were strangers in the land of Egypt . . ." (Leviticus 19, 33-34).

Again, in connection with business dealings, the Torah has this to say: "Just balances, just weights (and honest measures) shall ye have: (for) I am the Lord your God who brought you out of the land of Egypt." (*Ibid.*, 36).

When an Israelite had to sell himself because of poverty, his fellow Israelite was forbidden to make him serve as a slave. Why? "For they are My servants, whom I brought forth out of the land of Egypt; they shall not be sold as bondsmen." (Leviticus 25, 42).

Similarly the Exodus implied a certain kind of treatment of the weak or underprivileged: "Thou shalt not pervert the justice due to the stranger or to the fatherless; nor take the widow's raiment to pledge. But thou shalt remember that thou wast a bondsman in Egypt, and the Lord thy God redeemed thee thence . . ." (Deuteronomy 24, 17-18).

Even the act of eating has its relationship to the Exodus experience. The Jew was to eat kosher food only, so that every time he ate he would be reminded that he was holy, in a special relationship with God: "For I am the Lord thy God. I took thee up from the land of Egypt to be Thy God, so that ye may be holy, for I am holy." (Leviticus 11, 45, culminating all of chapter 11).

To live by the Exodus and to internalize its perspective, the Jew symbolically relives it in sacred ceremony. On Passover, for example, the Jew reenacts the Exodus—from eating the *matzah,* the bread of affliction, and tasting *maror,* the bitter herb with the wormwood taste of slavery and genocide, to drinking the wine of exultation and redemption. (This last is what Jesus was doing at the Last Supper.) Similarly, on the feast of the Tabernacles, Jews move into *succoth,* or portable booths, and live there as their fathers did millenia earlier when they marched through the desert after the flight from Egypt.

Living by the Light of the Ancient Covenant

From the pagan middle-bronze age of Abraham (with its worship of many gods) down to this very day, Jews have lived by the light of the ancient covenant. In the days of the kings and prophets, when the Jews lived in an agricultural society, responding to God's covenant meant (among other things) that every seven years debts were canceled and bondsmen were set free, so that no permanent poor class would be created (see Deuteronomy 15, 1-15). It also meant (at a time when land was the only source of income) that, in each generation, land would be redistributed so that every Jew was guaranteed the income to live (see Leviticus 25, 8-18).

Much later, when civilization changed from an agricultural to an urban one, and when most Jews lived in the Diaspora and were engaged in trade, the covenant had to be lived by in new ways. These were illuminated by the rabbis, who interpreted the implications of the Exodus for their own time as the prophets had done for theirs. Such developments were possible because Judaism believes that it is not only revelation from above (either direct or through the intermediary of the prophets) that reveals to us the will of God. The mind of man, operating with sincerity, holy purpose and wisdom can also discern the implications of God's concern for humanity. So rabbis asked such questions as: What is a just price? At what point does the profit margin become exploitative or excessive? By applying their judgment to contemporary questions, they tried to set up new and just limits. A concrete case in the Talmud is: Can a laborer quit his job to get better pay (or, in contemporary terms, can he strike?). Yes, is the rabbinical answer: "For unto Me are the children of Israel servants"—*i.e.,* they are not servants to other men (Leviticus 25, 55). A man who cannot strike to better his conditions is a servant, a slave, not a free man. And only a free man is capable of living up to God's covenant.

Judaism: Halachah (the Law)

From what has already been said, it can be seen that the central characteristic of Judaism—the Law, or *halachah*—is not simply a law; it is the Jewish way. (*Halachah* literally means walking, or the way.) *Halachah* is the application of the central theological beliefs of Judaism to *all* of life. It is living in the light of God's concern. Similarly the Torah, the Hebrew word for teachings, is not restricted solely to the Five Books of Moses, the Bible or any of the authoritative commentaries. Rather, it represents an entire civilization and way of life.

The Pharisees

It was the Pharisees who grasped this dynamic nature of revelation. It was they who taught that God wants the *heart* of man to serve Him, so that forms and institutions could change to express the service of the heart. They taught that God was wherever men were; wherever they met, spoke or thought of Him (see Ethics of the Fathers, chapter 3, paragraph 3, 4). The Pharisees served as carpenters, shoemakers, blacksmiths, woodcutters, farmers, businessmen and teachers. They showed the way themselves by serving in the secular and not becoming religious functionaries. This stood them in good stead when the great crisis came for the Jews with the destruction of the Temple.

Destruction of the Temple (70 A.D.)

When the Second Temple was destroyed in 70 A.D., the Jewish people lost both their central sanctuary and the heart of the sacred service. Although a part of the Jewish community continued to live in the land of Israel, Jewish life in its broadest sense shifted to the Diaspora. In the two hundred years that followed, repeated wars with Rome further weakened the fabric of life in Israel, and the intellectual and religious leadership passed to Babylonia. Some Jews reacted to the loss of the Temple with a kind of asceticism. Some called for an end to celebration. Some spoke of giving up family life. Still others wondered if any aspect of sacred tradition could continue, or whether the people of Israel had become, in effect, dry bones. Indeed the Jewish-Christian community finally withdrew from the Jewish community, convinced by the destruction of the Temple that Jewish life had come to an end.

The Diaspora and Rabbinic Leadership

The rabbinic leadership responded differently, however. They believed that God's promises were to be trusted, and that therefore Israel would not die. Furthermore, if the Jews were in exile, then the *Shechina* (or the Divine Presence) was in exile with them. While there was no longer a sacrificial system, there were still good deeds to be done, and atonement could be achieved through repentance of the heart. The synagogue—the Jewish house of prayer and assembly—located wherever Jews were, would be a "minor Temple." Thus the rabbis' response to the tragedy of 70 A.D. was to affirm life even while mourning, and to insure the fact that marriage and family life continued. At every marriage ceremony, a glass is broken to symbolize the fact that joy is not complete and cannot be until Israel and the Temple are restored. But married life and joy are affirmed. The destruction of the Temple should not crush man. Rather, they said: "On the day that the Temple was destroyed, the Messiah was born." Tradition and faith were deepened in the fires of tribulation and good deeds, prayer and sacred service were internalized. The net result was that Israel survived.

Shift from Sacramental Ceremony to Mitzvah (Performance of Commandments)

One might say that the destruction of the Temple did for Judaism what the inroads of modern culture have done for Catholicism: it led to a greater stress on personal participation, increased lay involvement, greater congregational response and making the secular sacred. The psychology and tone of the sacred system that had embraced the Temple was "sacramental"; the worshiper was more passive; grace tended to be dispensed by the priest. In other words, sacredness seemed to be, as it were, restricted to special places, and isolated from life. By comparison, the synagogue service which became more and more developed, involved the congregation directly. In addition, the spiritual values of Jewish tradition were internalized by shifting the emphasis from sacramental ceremonies to performance of commandments, or as it is called in Hebrew—*mitzvah*. Essentially untranslatable, the word *mitzvah* refers to a deed which fuses action and religious values in a single act. Thus, it can be ritual—like prayer; or it can be a secular or human act—such as helping a person in need, or doing an honest day's work, or giving charity. If done out of love and an awareness of God, it is a *mitzvah.* In this way, all of life became consecrated and the reverence for it expressed through the *mitzvot*. The result was that, where the prophets had done poorly, the rabbis succeeded brilliantly. The old idolatry was undermined, and this new religious value system won the hearts and minds of the Jewish masses. The people of Israel became more consistently faithful than ever before. And, although prophecy was at an end, the process of religious renewal continued apace.

And so Jews walked the way of the Diaspora, the way of the Exile. Except for a small community, the ancient land was left behind—left behind, but not forgotten. At burial and at birth, at weddings and at parties, the Temple is remembered and Jerusalem prayed for. After every meal, the religious Jew recites grace, and in it he says, "And rebuild Jerusalem the holy city speedily in our days. . . . May the Merciful One . . . lead us upright to our land. . . ." Similarly, every morning when he prays, he says, "May our eyes behold Your return, in mercy, to Zion."

The Talmud and the Responsa: Maimonides

The Exile defies generalization. Perhaps the only legitimate one is that the covenant was lived, and that the development of the tradition continued. From the third to the tenth centuries the academies of Babylonia superseded the seats of learning of Israel. During this period, they compiled the *Talmud*—the greatest repository of Jewish tradition, law and religious custom. It includes Bible commentary, legend, history, ethics, humor, medicine, astronomy and astrology, science and superstition and above all, a stunning gallery of religious character portraits. Thus oriental Jewry helped spawn Islam, even as it predecessor had influenced Christianity.

When the Talmud was completed, the search for new religious direction did not stop. People turned now to the rabbis and scholars for guidance. If a problem in life came up that the individual could not resolve himself, he went to the rabbi for guidance. The question he posed was called *sh'elah;* the rabbi's response, *t'shuvah.* The range of the Responsa was enormous because the range of Jewish life was so vast.

No problem was either too major or too trivial for the Responsa. Question: Should a community turn over one of its people to persecutors as a hostage-victim to save the rest of the community? Maimonides' answer was: If he is innocent—no. On the other hand: What do you do with a knife that was used to cut meat and was accidentally plunged into a cup of milk? (Jewish dietary law forbade the mixing of meat and dairy foods.) The response: Wash it.

From the tenth century on, the center of Jewish religious life moved to Europe: to France, Germany and Spain. Perhaps the finest moment came in Spain (13th-14th century) when religious tolerance, economic prosperity and cross-cultural contacts fused and then flowered in the so-called Golden Age of Spanish Jewry. The result was an extraordinary outburst of poetry, both secular and religious; Bible commentary; philosophy which sought to reconcile ancient philosophy with revelation, and was to deeply influence Christian thought; ethics; historical writing, and a great mystical literature. The classic work of this period was unquestionably Maimonides' *Mishneh Torah*, which was a topical summary and organization of Jewish tradition, a philosophy and method of law, as well as a legal encyclopedia.

The Golden Age came to an end, like other great periods of the Diaspora, with political repression, economic decline, the expulsion of many Jews and the forced conversion of others. In the process, the Responsa took on a more somber hue.

An example. A group of refugee Jewish women were about to be seized by pirates. Rather than submit to rape and slavery, they committed suicide. Is this to be judged an act of consecration and martyrdom? Or is the affirmation of life and opposition to suicide so basic to Jewish tradition that this act should not be praised and perhaps even condemned? Another question: What about a man converted under duress when others stood fast? How shall he be judged? Now that he has escaped to a free Jewish community, what if anything should be said to him about the past?

Hasidism

There is little doubt that, during the course of the Diaspora, many Jews were cut off from their community by voluntary or forced assimilation. Some movements separated themselves from the people of Israel. Such was the fate of early Samaritans, eighth to the tenth-century Karaites, and Frankists of the eighteenth century. More often, however, the function of new movements was the regeneration of the spirit. As time and circumstances change, a gap grows between the word and the listener, between the covenant and the actual life of the people. As long as religious vitality remains in the people, a new movement arises to restore the vision and to relate anew past tradition to the present. One of the greatest of these movements proved to be *Hasidism,* with its emphasis on joy and mysticism, which flourished from the latter part of the eighteenth century onwards. Characteristically, such a movement brings conflict and controversy, but its absence would mean death of the soul. "For want of vision, a people perish."

Modern Religious Development: Orthodox, Conservative, Reform

The modern situation in particular has created a radically new era for Judaism and represents a sharp break from medieval times. With the growth of democracy and industrialization came the end of political Christendom, the beginning of secular culture and the emancipation of Jewry. This modernization has been the increasingly dominant experience of the Jewish community since 1789. Perhaps the most striking development was within the religious framework—*i.e.,* the emergence of the three trends: Orthodox, Conservative and Reform. Another development was the degree to which many Jews were passionately swept up in universal movements—humanitarianism, liberalism, revolutionary enterprises, and even agrarianism. There was likewise an extraordinary outburst of cultural creativity which led to the flowering of Yiddish literature, the revival of Hebrew, and a vast Jewish scholarship in the languages of Western Europe. And, finally, there was Zionism which flowered in 1948 with the founding of the State of Israel.

More Recent Developments: Zionism, New Self-image

The capacity of Jews to live in response to the great events in history (even to such an event as the Holocaust) is at this very moment generating new directions in Judaism. The result is a new ferment, a rethinking of inherited positions and a renewed search for religious meaning and unity.

There is also a new self-acceptance, a new self-image. Many Jews, who in their deep involvement in general culture and universal concerns were formerly embarrassed by their Jewishness, tend now to take it for granted or to accept it freely. As a consequence, there is a new openness to tradition and a search for living values that can be extracted from it. There is a new willingness to question whether too much has been accepted uncritically under rubric of modernism. At the same time, there has been a significant decline in insularity, and "the siege mentality." Even to the Orthodox Jew, the completion of emancipation has been a proof that his values and beliefs can be maintained within the framework of new cultural developments. In fact, if anything, there is a quickening concern lest in saying nay to what he believes to be the excesses of modernism, he does not lose touch with contemporary life or find himself alienated from the rest of the community. One might therefore say that the Jewish Orthodox community is at much the same stage of the cycle that Catholicism was at after the peak of defensiveness under Pope Pius the Ninth (Pio Nono) was passed.

Role of Judaism in Israel

In evaluating the present state of Judaism, it seems clear that the bulk of Jews will remain in the Diaspora and that Jewish religious life will be poly-centered in the future. It seems equally clear that the reborn Israel will be a major focus of both religious and cultural inspiration. (For example, a new holiday of thanksgiving for the creation of the State is gradually being created by folk and religious authority—the first new Jewish holiday in almost two millenia.) As a consequence, there is a profound theological upheaval taking place in Israel. Quite simply, it is the shift from the dilemmas of powerlessness to the dilemmas of power: how to exercise power morally, within the context of ambiguities which all nation states are heir to; how Judaism can consecrate national life without becoming a mere yea-sayer to the State; and, ultimately, how to reconcile the secular with the religious. The issue of religious service and its value in the political and secular areas of human life are beginning to generate great concern in Israel. Though the *halachah* has always sought to consecrate "the everyday," it is almost two thousand years since it has had to give guidance and counsel within the context of a political reality where national and security interests are at stake.

It remains to be seen whether Judaism can fuse both the prophetic critique of the use of power and the halachic covenantal guidance in the day-to-day exercise of the responsibilities of power. But, from any point of view, the experience of Israel has drawn (and will continue to draw) Jews of all types together in human fellowship and in religious concern.

Conclusion

If a general truth can be stated at this point it is that, for the Jewish people and for the Jewish faith, today is the best of times and it is the worst of times. Confusion and perplexity, assimilation and disintegration vie with tremendous new forces of reintegration and religious inspiration. Erstwhile atheistic collective settlements have painfully and haltingly developed new prayer books for religious services. Orthodox rabbis have given up life in cloistered study to become social workers in the city. The secularist general who led the recapture of Jerusalem wept before the Western Wall of the Temple, but said he knew not why. In America, intermarriage rates of Jews are at an all-time high, more Jews are studying Torah full-time than at any period of Jewish history. Jews have never been so listened to as they are at this moment of American culture—yet few of the Jews who speak are truly steeped in the tradition.

The Talmud says that such a welter of destruction and creation characterizes the Messianic time. There are those of us who dare hope that the Jew will find the way. Perhaps, in the new world which is being born, the travail and path of the Jew will be of significance to others who seek to walk the covenantal way with God and man: so that we will all light each other's way and that in His light, we will all see light.

JEWISH WORSHIP

Rabbi Max J. Routtenberg

Prayer: Source and Nature

In his introduction to *The Authorized Daily Prayer Book,* the late Chief Rabbi of the British Empire, Dr. Joseph H. Hertz, wrote: "Prayer is an instinct that springs eternally from man's unquenchable faith in a living God . . . it ranges from half-articulate petition for help in distress to highest adoration, from confession of sin to jubilant expression of joyful fellowship with God, from thanksgiving to the solemn resolve to do His will as if it were our will. Prayer is a Jacob's ladder joining earth to heaven; and, as nothing else, wakens in the children of men the sense of kinship with their Father on High."

The prayers of Judaism, evolved out of Jewish religious and historic experience, are a multi-patterned mosaic of thanksgiving and praise, petition and confession, affirmation and reminiscence, study and meditation. Their principal source is in the Sacred Scriptures, *i.e.,* in the words of patriarchs and prophets, psalmists and seers. Through the ages, the treasury of prayer has been enriched by the compositions of rabbis, sages, poets and mystics, all of whom gave voice to their souls' deepest yearnings and expressed both the pathos and majesty of Israel's role in human history.

Liturgy

In the course of time, many of these prayers, which were individual and spontaneous in the origin, have been arranged and incorporated into a fixed liturgy by rabbinical authority. The text of the liturgy for daily and Sabbath worship is called the *siddur,* meaning "order of service." The text of the liturgy for the High Holy Days and for the Pilgrim Festivals (Sukkot, Shavuot and the Passover) is called *mahzor,* meaning "cycle of service."

Based on the original script delivered on closed-circuit television.

Periods and Places of Worship

Jewish tradition has established three periods of worship for each day of the week—morning, afternoon and evening. The devotions of the morning are called *shaharit;* of the afternoon, *minha;* of the evening, *maariv.* On Sabbaths, New Moons and Festivals, additional prayers are appended to the morning service, and are called *mussaf.* A Jew may recite his prayers at a congregational service which must consist of not less than ten adult males (thirteen years of age qualifies one for religious responsibilities); or he may recite his prayers privately, wherever he may be. Tradition, however, has emphasized the importance of joining with a congregation in prayer, and has regarded public worship as more praiseworthy than private devotions.

Symbolic Ritual

To heighten the mood of prayer and to arouse the spiritual receptivity of the worshiper, Jewish tradition has prescribed the wearing of certain symbols during morning prayers. One is the prayer shawl, called the *tallit.* This garment, usually of wool or silk, is draped around the shoulders and must have fringes in the four corners, called *tzitzit,* to satisfy the ritual requirement. The other is the phylacteries, called *tefillin.* The phylacteries consist of two parts. The first is wound seven times around the left arm and three times around the middle finger; the second is draped around the head. Each phylactery has a container in which there is a special parchment with an inscription from a passage in the Torah. These ritual symbols are worn by adult males, whether at a public service or in private. On Sabbaths and Festivals, the phylacteries are not worn, only the *tallit.*

Language of Prayer

The basic language of Jewish worship is Hebrew, though the prayer book also contains some prayers in Aramaic—the language of the people in ancient Palestine and Babylonia. Many modern prayer books include translations (alongside the Hebrew text) into the language of the land in which they are published.

Jewish Public Worship: The Synagogue

One of the basic features of Jewish public worship is the public reading of the Torah, or the Five Books of Moses. During the course of the year, the entire Torah is read consecutively, portion by portion. A reading is held each Sabbath in the morning and afternoon; each

Monday and Thursday; on the New Moon; on Festivals, and on fast days. Readings from the Prophets and the Later Writings are generally limited to Sabbaths and Festivals.

To get a clear picture of what goes on in the traditional synagogue, let us imagine ourselves at a public service on the Sabbath. The men are seated together, whereas the women occupy a separate section. (In Reform and Conservative Synagogues there is mixed seating.) The men are wearing their prayer shawls and their heads are covered, usually with a skull cap, called *yarmulke* or *kippa*. They are holding their prayer books and they are reciting their prayers (*davening*). On a raised platform, *bimah*, sometimes in the center of the synagogue, sometimes at the far end of the room, stands the leader of the service, the cantor or *hazzan*, who has been especially trained to chant the service in the traditional mode. He may himself sing a musical setting for a prayer, or he may lead the congregation in a chant.

Three Focal Points in the Service: (a) The Shema

There are three focal points in the service. The first is the *Shema*, the oldest formulation of the Jewish faith and the most sacred prayer in the liturgy. It is recited twice daily, in the morning and in the evening, with deep devotion and concentration. It consists of four paragraphs, three of which are from the Book of Numbers. The best known are the first two paragraphs:

> Hear O Israel, the Lord is our God, the Lord is One.
> Thou shalt love the Lord thy God with all thy heart, with all thy soul, and with all thy might. And these words which I command thee this day shall be in thy heart. Thou shalt teach them diligently unto thy children, speaking of them when thou sittest in thy house, when thou walkest by the way, when thou liest down and when thou risest up. And thou shalt bind them for a sign upon thine hand, and they shall be for frontlets between thine eyes. And thou shalt write them upon the doorposts of thy house and upon thy gates.

In these paragraphs can be found the basic catechism of the Jewish religion: God is One and Indivisible. This is monotheism in its purest expression. It includes the belief in God as the Creator of the Universe (one world) and as the Father of all Mankind (one humanity). It declares that the relationship of man to God is one of love, to be striven after with heart and soul and might. It is man's duty to teach the love of God and to implant that love in the hearts of his children. To dramatize God's love, he shall use certain rituals and symbols, such as the phylacteries and the fringes, as well as the *mezuzah* which is placed upon the doorpost of the house and which likewise contains a prayer written on parchment. For, as an ancient sage has said: "He who places the *mezuzah* on the door, the *tefillin* on his head and arm, and the fringes on his garment (the *tallit*), the chances are strongly in his favor that he will not sin."

(b) The Amidah

The second focal point of the service is the Standing Prayer, or the *amidah*. On weekdays, this prayer is referred to as "The Eighteen," the *Shemoneh Esreh,* so designated because of the eighteen benedictions of which it was originally composed. (A 19th benediction was added at a later period.) The first three and last three benedictions of the *Amidah* consist of prayers of praise and thanksgiving. The middle section contains prayers petitioning God for wisdom, for health, for prosperity, for the restoration of Zion and for peace. On the Sabbath and Festivals, these thirteen petitionary prayers are replaced by one special prayer which deals with the holiness of the day.

The entire congregation rises for the *Amidah* and recites it silently, with intense concentration and devotion. The Cantor then chants the entire *Amidah* in his turn. During this repetition, a special prayer called "Sanctification," *Kedushah,* is recited. Its central theme is: "Holy, holy, holy, is the Lord of Hosts; the whole earth is full of His glory."

(c) Reading of the Torah

The third focal point of the service is the reading of the weekly portion from the Torah. The Scroll is taken from the Holy Ark, the *aron hakodesh,* and, after appropriate prayers and processional, is brought to the Reader's desk. The Torah Reader is a man expertly trained in the correct reading and chanting of the Torah text.

The Scriptural reading is divided into seven sections, and seven adult male members of the congregation are called to the desk in turn for the honor of blessing each individual section. This honor is called "Ascent," *aliyah.* When a boy reaches the age of 13, he signalizes his religious majority by being called to the Torah for an *aliyah,* which is usually followed by his chanting a selection from the Prophets, called *haftorah.*

At the conclusion of the Torah reading, a special prayer is recited, the *kaddish.* This is probably one of the best-known prayers in the liturgy. It may be compared to the *Magnificat* or the *Pater Noster,* to both of which it bears a close resemblance in ideas. It is composed in Aramaic and is recited at the conclusion of each major section of the service. In the course of time, mourners who attended memorial services became accustomed to reciting this prayer, and for this reason it became popularly known as "the mourner's prayer."

The basic requirements of Jewish worship are deemed fulfilled by the recitation of the *Shema* and the *Amidah,* and by the reading of the Torah.

Other Prayers

However, there are many other prayers that adorn and embellish Jewish worship. For example, numerous Psalms are interspersed through the liturgy, as well as later compositions of hymns of praise and adoration.

Each of the services concludes with the great prayer of Adoration, the *Alenu,* the closing words of which contain the Messianic hope:

> Let all the inhabitants of the world perceive and know that unto Thee every knee must bend, every tongue pledge loyalty. Before Thee, O Lord, let them bow in worship and give honor to Thy glorious Name. May they all accept the yoke of Thy kingdom, and do Thou reign over them speedily and for ever and ever. For the Kingdom is Thine and to all eternity Thou wilt reign in glory, as it is written in Thy Torah, the Lord shall reign for ever and ever; and it is said, The Lord shall be King over all the earth: in that day the Lord shall be One and His Name One.

ASPECTS OF JEWISH THEOLOGY: PART I

Rabbi Eugene B. Borowitz

Absence of Dogma

Judaism has no dogmas. That, I guess, is the one dogmatic truth on which all Jewish scholars would agree. Yet, even so, there are those who would insist that there have been certain beliefs so central to Judaism and so widely accepted that they are, in fact, the equivalent of dogmas. The first thing I must do, then, is to make clear that, in my discussion of Jewish tradition, I'm speaking for myself alone, and that the only authority I have is what my years of study have brought to these interpretations.

I suppose that the main reason Judaism is something of an undogmatic religion is that the Bible itself is not, as Jews understand it, a book of dogma. (Incidentally, when I speak of the Bible, I mean the Hebrew Scriptures. This is what in Christian terms would be called "The Old Testament.") This Bible is not a book concerned with abstractions, with philosophic statements about Truth, or even with trying to delineate obligatory beliefs. Rather, it is a book of history, of law, of poetry, of criticism and of practical wisdom. We Jews read the Bible within the context of the rabbinic tradition. In other words, it is the ancient rabbis who have given us guidance as to what the Bible is really trying to say, and have helped us to understand it in all its complexity and difficulty. Occasionally, in the writings of those rabbis who lived between the century before and the first few centuries after the time of Jesus, one does come across dogmatic statements. Yet it is not until well into the Middle Ages that one encounters a sustained effort to put into clear-cut form what seem to be those beliefs that lie at the heart of and are essential to Judaism.

Based on the original script delivered on closed-circuit television.

Moses Maimonides

One of the greatest medieval Jewish thinkers, Moses Maimonides, was outstanding in his attempts not only to formulate the truths of Jewish faith, but also to clarify what it was that Jewish law required of Jews. Already as a young man, Maimonides tried to set down what he believed were the essential beliefs of the Jewish religion, and this is about the closest thing we have had in Jewish tradition to what may be called "a creed." Here, in the shortened form in which it appears in our prayer book, is that creed, generally known as the Thirteen Articles of Faith:

> I believe with perfect faith that the Creator, blessed be his Name, is the Author and Guide of everything that has been created, and that He alone has made, does make, and will make, all things.
>
> I believe with perfect faith that the Creator, blessed be his Name, is a unity and that there is no unity in any manner like unto His, and that He alone is our God, who was, is, and will be.
>
> I believe with perfect faith that the Creator, blessed be his Name, is not a body, and that He is free from all the properties of matter, and that He has not any form whatsoever.
>
> I believe with perfect faith that the Creator, blessed be his Name, is the first and last.
>
> I believe with perfect faith that to the Creator, blessed be his Name, and to Him alone, it is right to pray, and that it is not right to pray to any being besides Him.
>
> I believe with perfect faith that all the words of the prophets are true.
>
> I believe with perfect faith that the prophecy of Moses, our teacher, was true, and that he was the chief of the prophets, both of those that preceded and those that followed.
>
> I believe with perfect faith that the whole Torah, now in our possession, is the same that was given to Moses, our teacher.
>
> I believe with perfect faith that this Torah will not be changed, and that there will never be any other law from the Creator, Blessed be his Name.
>
> I believe with perfect faith that the Creator, Blessed be his Name, knows every deed of the children of men and all their thoughts, as it is said, 'It is He that fashioneth the hearts of them all, that giveth heed to all their works.
>
> I believe with perfect faith that the Creator, Blessed be his

Name, rewards those that keep his commandments and punishes those that transgress them.

I believe with perfect faith in the coming of the Messiah; and, though he tarry, I will wait daily for his coming.

I believe with perfect faith that there will be a revival of the dead at the time when it shall please the Creator, Blessed be his Name, and exalted be his fame for ever and ever. *

Reaction

Shortly after the time that Maimonides had made this creed public, there was great disagreement about it in the Jewish religious community. Indeed, some of the later Jewish medieval philosophers radically revised what Maimonides had said—one of them going even so far as to insist that the belief in the coming of the Messiah was a desirable but not a necessary belief in Judaism. This shows the length to which Judaism often goes in being undogmatic. Today, if anything, the situation is even more complicated. Jews are divided into Orthodox, those who substantially represent a continuation of Jewish tradition as we know it; Conservative, those who want to maintain tradition and yet modernize it; and Reform, those who are prepared to make more radical changes in Judaism. In addition, we have large numbers of Jews who are not concerned with *any* interpretation of Judaism. Thus diversity has increased rather than decreased.

Unity of Tradition, in Spite of Diversity

And yet, in spite of this, there is a sense of unity to Jewish tradition. Again and again, for example, Maimonides speaks of "The Creator"; for, fundamental to Jewish faith, is the unqualified acknowledgement of the sovereignty of the One and Only God. This perhaps may best be understood when viewed in terms of the continuous fight against the paganism with which bibical man was surrounded. Pagan man conceived of the world as diverse and plural; he could not see underlying it any overriding sense of unity. On the other hand, the Jew believed that there was something unified about the world in which he lived, and that this unity transcended all the divisions which can be found in life. It is this strong sense of the authority of one God; He who has an

---

*From *The Authorized Daily Prayer Book,* J. H. Hertz, editor. Shapiro, Vallentine & Co., 1959.

absolute right to our allegiance, to command us, to guide us, which distinguishes Judaism from paganism. It is this sense of unity, too, which lies behind what is often called the watchword of the Jewish faith, the *Shema:* "Sh'ma Yis-ra-el, A-do-noy, E-lo-hay-noo, A-do-noy E-had." "Hear, O Israel, the Lord, our God, the Lord is One."

Who and What is God; Relation to Him.

To the Jew, it is not simply true that there is a unity behind all things and that this unity transcends all of Nature, but rather that God is a commanding presence who, by His very nature, comes before man and requires of him that he should live in certain ways. Because God is one, so man must be one. Because God is one and therefore always God, so man must always be true to God and at no time deviate from Him. This is the root, the core idea of Judaism: namely, that man must devote himself to God.

The Bible does not offer much proof for the existence of God. (Although we read on occasion in rabbinic literature of debates that the rabbis had with the philosophers, of questions asked by heretics, and of sporadic efforts to demonstrate God's existence, somehow all of this is rather tangential to the Jewish tradition.) Instead, Jews have known about God through historic experience. The Exodus from Egypt and the freeing of the Jewish people had an immediacy for the individual Jew which, despite all the claims of the pagan gods, made him realize that indeed there was only one God, above and beyond and running through all things. And, as the Bible makes clear, this realization that first grew out of the Exodus experience was renewed for Jews again and again.

The whole question of who and what is God comes to a climax in the writings of that anonymous prophet of the Exile whom today we customarily call "the Second Isaiah." The greatest of the biblical theologians, he is not a dispassionate thinker. If anything, he is an enraptured poet who has set his faith before us with a beauty which is almost as astonishing as his insight and understanding. Following is a selection from Isaiah, Chapter 45, 5-25 in which he speaks to us of the One, the Only, the historic God:

> I am the Lord, and there is none else. Beside me there is no God. I have girded thee, though thou hast not known Me; that they may know from the rising of the sun and from the west, that there is none beside Me. I am the Lord, and there is none else. I

form the light and create darkness; I make peace, and create evil;
I am the Lord that doeth all these things . . . .

For thus sayeth the Lord that created the heavens, He is God
that formed the earth and made it. He established it; He created it
not a waste; He formed it to be inhabited. I am the Lord, and
there is none else. I have not spoken in secret, in a place of the
land of darkness . . . .

Look unto Me and be ye saved, all the ends of the earth; for I
am God, and there is none else. By myself have I sworn—the
word is gone forth from My mouth in righteousness, and shall
not come back—that unto Me every knee shall bow, every tongue
shall swear. Only in the Lord, shall one say of Me, is victory and
strength. Even to Him shall men come in confusion, all they that
were incensed against Him. In the Lord shall all the seed of Israel
be justified and shall glory.

God's Relation to Man: The General Covenant.

Now, what astonishes, what overwhelms, the biblical writers is that
this great, this transcendant God relates to man. He is a God, who, to
use the biblical term, makes a "covenant" with man. He lets man know
who He is and that He cares. This sense man has that he and God
stand in partnership, that finite, indeed animal-like though he is, he
nonetheless is related to that God—this sense lies at the heart of biblical
faith.

It is interesting that the biblical authors use a term like "covenant" to
describe the relationship between God and man. We know from many
samples of Near Eastern literature, as well as from the Bible itself, that
the word *brit* (covenant) is a legal term which was commonly used in
ancient jurisprudence. It seems fair to assume, therefore, that what the
biblical authors were trying to convey by using this term is that man's
relationship to God is a mutually binding one. God demands of man
that he shall follow His law by living his life in certain ways. At the
same time He, God, promises that He will be with man, and that He
will guide man in the course of his existence. So that what is established
is a situation in which finite man is linked to a transcendent cause, and
can feel himself part of a cosmic plan.

It should be pointed out at this stage that, according to Jewish tradition, the covenant is not viewed as having been entered into with the
Jews alone, but rather with all mankind; with Adam who was not a Jew
and who, as the first man, was the archetype of all future humanity.
Thus God came to Adam in the Garden of Eden and gave him certain

commandments: "Be fruitful and multiply"; "Subdue the earth"; "Name the beasts." In return, God saw to it that Adam was abundantly supplied with the wherewithal for survival.

This covenant with all mankind, of whom Adam was the progenitor, was repeated in the story of Noah. God, so the Bible tells us, having become exasperated with men and their behavior, brought on the Flood. But, before doing this, He made certain that one righteous man, Noah, would be saved, for righteousness is God's concern. It is not punishment that He desires, but only that men be good. So that, when He brought Noah safely out of the ark, He made a covenant with him, once again reiterating (though in somewhat different and more concrete fashion) His mutual relationship with man. We find this stated in Genesis, Chapter 9:

> And God blessed Noah and his sons, and said to them, "Be fruitful and multiply and replenish the earth. And the fear of you and the dread of you shall be upon every beast of the earth and upon every fowl of the air . . . . Every moving thing that liveth shall be for food for you; as the green herb have I given you all. Only flesh with the life thereof, which is the blood thereof, shall ye not eat. And surely your blood of your lives will I require; at the hand of every beast will I require it; and at the hand of man, even at the hand of every man's brother, will I require the life of man. Whoso sheddeth man's blood, by man shall his blood be shed; for in the image of God made He man.
>
> "As for Me, behold I establish My covenant, with you, and with your seed after you . . . . I have set My bow in the cloud, and it shall be for a token of a covenant between Me and the earth . . . . so that I will remember My covenant which is between Me and you and every living creature of all flesh; and the waters shall no more become a flood to destroy all flesh . . . ."

Specific Covenant with Abraham

But man, being a creature of foolishness and willfulness, continued to sin. Therefore, God chose to make still another covenant—this one of a different order, however. This time it was with Abraham, the first Jew and the progenitor of the Chosen People, Israel. This covenant he was later to renew with Isaac and then with Jacob. In thus singling out a particular group of humanity, the Jews, and making a covenant directly with them, God was in effect expressing his reservations about mankind in general and making the Jews, so to speak, the repository of

His commandments and the conscience of all people. So that, when we speak of the Jews, we are speaking of this people, bound in special covenant to the Lord.

Many of the themes involved in this Jewish covenant with God are summed up in the latter chapters of Deuteronomy, particularly Chapters 29 and 30:

> You stand this day, all of you, before the Lord, your God, your tribes, your elders and your officials, even all the men of Israel, your children, your wives, and the stranger within your camp— from woodchopper to waterdrawer—to enter into the covenant of the Lord, your God, and into His oath which the Lord, your God, is concluding with you this day; to the end that He may establish you this day as His people, and be your God as he swore to your fathers, Abraham, Isaac and Jacob . . . . Surely this commandment which I enjoin upon you this day is not too hard for you, nor is it far off. It is not in heaven that you should say: "Who among us can go up to heaven and bring it to us, and impart it to us, so that we may observe it?" Neither is it beyond the sea, that you should say: "Who among us can cross to the other side of the sea and get it for us, and impart it to us, so that we may observe it?" No, the word is very close to you, in your mouth, and in your heart, so that you may observe it.
>
> See, I have set before you this day life and prosperity, death and adversity. For I command you this day to love the Lord, your God, to walk in His ways, and to keep His commandments and His laws and His ordinances; then you will thrive and multiply, and the Lord, your God shall bless you in the land which you are about to enter and possess. But, if your heart turns away, and you give no heed, and are lured into the worship and service of other gods, I declare to you this day that you shall certainly perish; you shall not long endure on the soil which you are crossing the Jordan to enter and possess. I call heaven and earth to witness against you this day, that I have put before you life and death, blessing and curse; therefore choose life so that you and your offspring may live; to love the Lord, your God, to heed His voice and to hold fast to Him; so that you shall have long life and may dwell in the land which the Lord, your God, swore to Abraham, to Isaac and to Jacob, to give them.

What an extraordinary thing it is that the One transcendent God wants man to have life, prosperity, happiness, length of days! This God who covenants with man loves man. He cares for him. And that is why what He asks of man is that man shall love Him. And that is why, according to Jewish tradition, God's love for man and God's love for Israel must be understood hand-in-hand—*i.e.,* that God covenants with the Jewish people because he cares for *all* mankind; because he wants an exemplar people, a witness, to make it known who He is and what He cares for. All men can and should know God; that is what the covenant of Noah was all about, for God cares for all of mankind. But, because man chose to go his own arrogant, rebellious way, God finally chose a special people. And what He expects of this special people is that they give him a special love.

Men and God Bound Together

What "covenant" then finally means is the love of God for man responded to by man's love for God. The commandments are there; the discipline is required. But we do not follow them simply because He has commanded us to do so, but because He is what He is and we love Him.

The Psalmists summed up this view of man and God and their relationship to one another in Psalm 8, a psalm of David:

Oh, Lord, our Lord, how glorious is Thy name in all the earth, whose majesty is rehearsed above the heavens. Out of the mouths of babes and sucklings hast Thou founded strength, because of Thine adversaries; that Thou might still the enemy and the avenger. When I behold Thy heavens, the work of Thy fingers, the moon and the stars which Thou hast established; what is man that Thou art mindful of him? And the son of man, that Thou thinkest of him? Yet Thou hast made him but little lower than the angels, and hast crowned him with glory and honor. Thou hast made him to have dominion over the works of Thy hand; Thou hast put all things under his feet: sheep and oxen, all of them, yea, and the beasts of the field; the fowl of the air, and the fish of the sea; whatsoever passes through the paths of the seas. Lord, our Lord, how glorious is Thy name in all the earth.

Thus, mankind and God are bound together in a covenant; and, though some men are bound to Him in a special way, no man is left out. It is a glorious vision of man. It depends upon a glorious vision of God. That, as *I* understand it, is the Hebrew tradition of man and God bound together in sacred covenant.

ASPECTS OF JEWISH THEOLOGY: PART II
Rabbi Eugene B. Borowitz

Jewish Religious Thought and Original Sin

There is debate among scholars about almost every aspect of the history of Jewish religious thought. Yet I think it is fair to say that most of them would agree that classical Judaism, although it may have flirted with the idea of original sin, never actually embraced it. True, if one looks back over Jewish religious tradition and, in particular, at the Book of Genesis, one discovers certain aspects of sin that appear to be viewed as being almost congenital to man. On the other hand, Jewish tradition has always argued that man could finally dominate and change his sinful nature. Since this whole question is bound up with the Jewish concept of redemption, and is crucial to an understanding of Israel's role in the history of mankind and to the ultimate hope in all of us, I think it important that we consider it for a moment.

In the Bible we find a considerable concern with sin, to say the least. In fact, one might even argue that the Bible is devoted to sin, seeing that the subject is dealt with on almost every page. The reason for this is almost certainly that sin represents rebellion against God. God cannot rule, God cannot be Himself, if by his actions man continually rejects both Him and His Will. Yet, for all of its sense of the seriousness and ubiquity of sin, Judaism—as has already been suggested—has never believed that man is hopelessly sinful. Take, for example, the story of Cain. In Genesis, Chapter 4, there appears what I think may be considered the key to the Jewish understanding of sin: "And God said to Cain, 'Why are you angry? And why is your countenance fallen? If you do well, shall it not be lifted up? And if you do not do well, sin couches at the door, and unto you is its desire; but you can rule over it.' " "You can rule over it"—*that* is the key verse. For, in Jewish tradition, man—though a sinner—can always repent, can always return to God.

Based on the original script delivered on closed-circuit television.

God's Covenant and Israel's Destiny

All this leads us to an interesting speculation. What is to be the destiny of mankind? What will happen to human beings if they continually rebel against God? It is here that God's covenant with Israel enters the picture—*i.e.,* it is Israel's function to save mankind from its own rebelliousness and sinfulness. This role is put into manifest form by that great biblical poet-theologian, The Second Isaiah. The following selections from Chapters 43 and 49 of his work speak of Israel's historic role as the "saving" people—

But now thus saith the Lord that created thee, O, Jacob, and He that formed thee, O Israel: 'Fear not, for I have redeemed thee; I have called thee by thy name; thou art mine. When thou passest through the waters, I will be with thee, and through the rivers, they shall not overflow thee. When thou walkest through the fire, thou shalt not be burned, neither shall the flame kindle upon thee. For I am the Lord, thy God, the holy one of Israel, thy Savior. . . .

'Ye are my witnesses,' saith the Lord, 'and My servant whom I have chosen; that ye may know and believe Me, and understand that I am He. Before Me there was no God formed; neither shall any be after Me. I, even I, am the Lord; and besides Me there is no Saviour. I have declared, and I have saved, and I have announced, and there was no strange God among you. Therefore ye are My witnesses,' saith the Lord, 'and I am God. Yea, since the day was, I am He, and there is none that can deliver out of My hand. I will work, and who can reverse it? . . ."

Listen, O isles, unto me, and hearken, ye peoples from far: the Lord hath called me from the womb; from the bowels of my mother hath He made mention of my name. And He hath made my mouth like a sharp sword, in the shadow of His hand hath He hid me. And He hath made me a polished shaft, in his quiver hath He concealed me. And He said unto me: 'Thou art my servant, Israel, in whom I will be glorified.' But I said: 'I have labored in vain; I have spent my strength for naught and vanity. Yet surely my right is with the Lord, and my recompense with my God.' 'And now,' saith the Lord that formed me from the womb to be His servant, to bring Jacob back to Him, and that Israel be gathered unto Him—for I am honorable in the eyes of the Lord, and my God has become my strength—'Yea,' he saith, 'it is too light a

thing that thou shouldest be My servant to raise up the tribes of
Jacob, and to restore the offspring of Israel; I will also give thee
for a light of the nations, that My salvation may be unto the end
of the earth.'

Yes, "A light unto the nations"—*that* is what the Hebrew people
understand its covenant with God to be. That not only do they have
the duty to worship and obey Him, but that, through their faithfulness
to God, *all* men will come to know and serve Him.

Israel's Obligations

Israel understands that it is to carry out its relationship to God, on
two separate levels, so to speak. First, and more obviously, by the
observance of His Law. In a way, the moment a Jew pronounces the
word "law," he wants to take it back. It has so many unpleasant connotations for people today, making us think of someone who gives us
a traffic ticket or catches us on our income-tax declaration. And this
is hardly the sense which the Jew has of Law. On the contrary, the
word "Law" has for him a far more joyous and happy meaning. In the
days of the Talmudic rabbis, for example, the Jews created a new holiday not prescribed in the Bible. They call it *Simhat Torah*—the
rejoicing in the Law. *This* is their understanding of that discipline.
Perhaps one can understand its function even better by thinking for
a moment of the Sabbath. True, the Sabbath is restrictive, and there
are things one may not do. Yet it is the day in which man breaks time,
in which he insists that nature can be made subject to the human will
and the human will dedicated to God. It is also the day in which the
family is joined together, the day on which one consecrates oneself to
worship and study. It is a day of discipline; but, through that discipline,
God is made known.

The second level—perhaps more difficult to understand—on which
the Jewish people carry out the covenant is by being a people, or what
the Bible calls "a nation." This term has certain political connotations
today which makes it not the best term to use. The Jews do not see themselves as a Church. Nor are they like the Buddhists, a brotherhood.
Instead, they tend to see themselves as an ethnic group, similar in most
ways to any other ethnic group—in terms of language, literature
and folkways—yet quite different in the sense that their being a people
or ethnic group is a cardinal feature of their relationship to God. They
were called into being as a people by God; they were taken out of Egypt
as a people, and as a people they were brought to Sinai and given the

Law which is their Constitution. Their function as a people is to endure through history, to bear witness through all of history to God's existence and laws. And, to carry out that function, they need to set up a community as an example to mankind of how to live in relationship to God. Which is why a part of their covenant with God has always included the land of Israel, why the land of Israel has always been central to the Jewish religion, and why Jewish prayers for 2000 years were filled with dreams of the return to the land of Israel.

I suppose it can seem strange to some that Jews in the United States are so deeply involved with their brothers in the land of Israel. But, even though Israeli Jews are organized as a state—indeed, I suppose, have to be a state in order to be able to function and survive as a community there—nonetheless, the concern of American Jews for their Israeli brothers is the result of the fact that they both share a covenantal purpose. In fact, the latter are trying to create that kind of society which the Bible talked of when it spoke of a covenant, *i.e.*, of a people which would be a light unto all nations. Therefore, Jews all over the world look today to Israel not only as the source of their covenant, but as the place where one Jewish community is trying (amidst all the difficulties, problems and confusions that spring from power, politics and money) to create nevertheless a covenantal nation.

Supreme Importance of the Covenantal Relationship

In all of the above, Judaism's understanding of its covenant relationship with God is implied. Indeed, already in the early chapters of God's meeting with Abraham, which appear in the Book of Genesis, we can see this is so. Take, for example, Chapter 17, in which God, the one transcendant Lord of the Universe, wishing to covenant with mankind so as to save them, addresses these words to his chosen, Abraham:

> When Abram[1] was 99 years old, the Lord appeared to Abram and said to him, 'I am El Shaddai.[2] Walk in My ways and be blameless. I will establish My covenant between Me and you, and I will make you exceedingly numerous.'

> Abram threw himself on his face, as God continued speaking to him, 'As for Me, this is My covenant with you: You shall be the

---

1. Abraham's name before God made His covenant with him, making him progenitor of the Jews.
2. God, the Almighty.

father of a multitude of nations. I will make you exceedingly fertile, and make nations of you; and kings shall come forth from you. I will maintain My covenant between Me and you, and your offspring to come, as an everlasting covenant throughout the ages, to be God to you and to your offspring to come. I give the land you sojourn in to you and your offspring to come, all the land of Canaan, as an everlasting possession. I will be their God.'

God further said to Abram, 'As for you, you shall keep My covenant, you and your offspring to come, throughout the ages. Such shall be the covenant which you shall keep, between Me and you and your offspring to follow: Every male among you shall be circumcised. You shall circumcise the flesh of your foreskin, and that shall be the sign of the covenant between Me and you. At the age of eight days, every male among you, throughout the generations, shall be circumcised, even the homeborn slave and the one bought from an outsider who is not of your seed. The slave that is born in your household or bought with your money must be circumcised. Thus shall My covenant be marked in your flesh as an everlasting pact. An uncircumcised male who does not circumcise the flesh of his foreskin—such a person shall be cut off from his kin; for he has broken My covenant.'

"An everlasting pact"; a covenant deeply cut into the flesh; a loyalty which is to continue from generation to generation. *That* is what the people of Israel have understood the covenant to be, as well as its responsibility to God throughout history. But there are two partners to the covenant. There is not only Israel, there is also God. And, if Israel does its part by working and waiting, it is assured that God in turn will do His part to fulfill Israel and carry out His purpose in history.

Concept of the Messiah

Which brings us to that great, that extraordinary, doctrine—the concept of the Messiah. And here one enters into one of the most controversial aspects of Jewish religious thought. It would be difficult, I think, to gain unanimity among Jewish scholars as to when and where the classic conception of the Messiah began in Jewish tradition. There are those who say that what we read in the Bible is merely a series of accounts of a good Jewish king who will one day arise. There are others who say, "No, these verses so well known to all of us, speak not simply of a good king, but of a day in which God Himself will announce the coming of a Messiah, an Anointed; that God will Himself make it possible for all men to live wholly and truly under His Law." These, I think, are the two sides of the Jewish understanding of the coming of the Messiah. On the one hand, he is, so to speak, only human; on the other, he is God's Anointed, he is God's Agent, the one who will lead mankind to His Kingdom.

Similarly, I think that it might be possible (although research is not unambiguous on this subject) to divide Jewish eschatological concerns into two levels: the days of the Messiah which are relatively human and natural, and an ensuing period—rather more extraordinary—which we might call the Kingdom of God. It is quite clear that by rabbinical times, *i.e.*, the several centuries before and the several centuries after Christ, the human and the eschatological became linked. And that they become as fundamental to traditional Judaism as any idea could be.

Rather than quote from the rabbis, it might be more interesting at this point to look at a summary of Maimonides, that great medieval Jewish thinker, who in the twelfth century set down in his Code of Law some of the ideas that were subsequently to influence Jewish thinking about the Messiah—

> Do not think that King Messiah will have to perform signs and wonders, bring anything new into being, revive the dead, or do similar things. It is not so. Rabbi Akibah was a great sage, a teacher of the *Mishnah*,[3] yet he was also the armor-bearer of Ben Kosibah.[4] He affirmed that the latter was King Messiah. He and all the wise men of his generation shared this belief until Ben Kosibah was slain in (his) iniquity, when it became known that he was not (the Messiah). Yet, the Rabbis had not asked him for a sign or token. The general principle is: this Law of ours with its statutes and ordinances (is not subject to change). It is for ever and all eternity; it is not to be taken away from. (Whoever adds aught to it, or takes away aught from it, or misinterprets it, and strips the commandments of their literal sense is an impostor, a wicked man, and a heretic.)

> If there arise a king from the House of David who meditates on the Torah, occupies himself with the commandments, as did his

3. A section of the Talmud consisting of a collection of oral laws edited *c.* 200 A.D. by Rabbi Judah Ha-Nasi.

4. Another name for Bar-Kokhba, famous Jewish revolutionary leader against the Romans.

ancestor David, observes the precepts prescribed in the Written and
the Oral Law, prevails upon Israel to walk in the way of the Torah
and to repair its breaches, and fights the battles of the Lord, it may
be assumed that he is the Messiah. If he does these things and suc-
ceeds, rebuilds the sanctuary on its site, and gathers the dispersed
of Israel, he is beyond all doubt the Messiah. He will prepare the
whole world to serve the Lord with one accord, as it is written:
For then will I turn to the people a pure language that they may
call upon the name of the Lord to serve Him with one consent
(Zeph. 3:9).

One thing that may appear surprising is how little Maimonides seemed
to know about what will happen in the days of the Messiah. And, while
it is fair to say that as a philosopher he was deliberately restraining himself from pure speculation, it is also true that there has not been great
concern in Jewish tradition with what will happen, either in the days
of the coming of the Messiah or in the days afterwards when the Kingdom of God will be established. Jewish tradition has been far more
concerned with the *"here and now."* One almost has the impression that
the great Jewish teachers did not want the believing Jew to spend too
much time worrying about the life of the world to come, for fear that
consequently he would not pay attention to what he had to do in the
world of the present. And, yet, some things are clear. First, it is the hope
that, when the Messiah comes, there will finally be peace and justice.
Second, that there will be the love of man for his neighbor. But, above
all, that there will be the love of God and the knowledge of God, in
ways that we now cannot understand and can only dimly perceive.

Life After Death; The Kingdom of God

One sign of the extraordinary fulfillment which the days of the
Messiah followed by the Kingdom of God will bring, of course, is the
theory of life after death. Here, too, Hebrew tradition has not been
terribly clear; and yet, it has been the classic faith of Jewish people
that God in His wisdom will see to it that the one inescapable human
experience—death—will ultimately be overcome. Similarly, during the
rabbinic period and in some places in the Bible, the doctrine is enunciated that there *will* be the resurrection of the dead.

The Jews have had this belief in the coming of the Messiah for many
centuries. It has been basic to their understanding of what it means to
be a man and to participate in history. It has been, too, the source of
their continuing hope. People often wonder how it has been possible

for such a small minority as the Jews, with so little practical effect upon the affairs of men, to have borne the persecution and oppression they have (in many climates and under many circumstances) and yet to have remained faithful to that covenant to which we have been continually referring. I think the answer is quite clear. It lies in the Jewish hope that the Messiah will come. Or, if one puts it in its furthest eschatological reach, that the day will come in which the Kingdom of God will be established on earth.

Jewish Hopes for Mankind

In this connection, it is worthwhile noting that a prayer, originally recited only on the Jewish New Year and expressing this Jewish sense of hope for mankind and human history, was transferred some centuries ago to the daily service. Closing, as it does, every Jewish service, this prayer almost seems to spell out what the Jews must do (in the here and now!) as they leave their prayers and take up their daily life:

> It is our duty to praise the Lord of all things, to ascribe greatness to Him who formed the world in the beginning, since He hath not made us like the nations of other lands, and hath not placed us like other families of the earth, since He hath not assigned unto us a portion as unto them, nor a lot as unto all their multitude. For we bend the knee and offer worship and thanks before the supreme King of Kings, the Holy One, Blessed be He, who stretched forth the heavens and laid the foundation of the earth, the seat of whose glory is in the heavens above, and the abode of whose might is in the loftiest heights. He is our God; there is none else: in truth, He is our King; there is none besides Him. As it is written in His Torah, 'And thou shalt know this day, and lay it to thine heart, that the Lord, He is God, in heaven above and upon the earth beneath: there is none else.'

> We therefore hope in thee, O Lord our God, that we may speedily behold the glory of Thy might, when Thou wilt remove the abominations from the earth, and heathendom will be utterly destroyed; when the world will be perfected under the Kingdom of the Almighty, and all the children of flesh will call upon thy Name; when Thou wilt turn unto thyself all the evildoers upon earth. Let all the inhabitants of the world perceive and know that unto Thee every knee must bow, every tongue must swear allegiance. Before Thee, O Lord our God, let them bow and worship;

and unto thy glorious Name let them give honor; let them all accept the yoke of Thy Kingdom, and do Thou reign over them speedily, and for ever and ever. For the Kingdom is Thine, and to all eternity Thou wilt reign in glory. As it is written in Thy Torah, 'The Lord shall reign for ever and ever.' And it is said, 'And the Lord shall be King over all the earth: in that day shall the Lord be one, and his Name one.'

Summary

Because God *is* one, there can only be one end to history. Because God cares for man and covenants with him, He will not let him go. Because God loves mankind, he has bound himself to the people of Israel and bound the people of Israel to Him, so that they may testify to Him and His reality and all of history. Thus the people of Israel— small, dispersed, beaten—remain God's faithful witness in history. So they understand themselves; so they understand their task and their duty. They are a strange people, the people of Israel. A people who have in their background and tradition the most diverse experiences; who have lived in tropical and temperate climates; under nomadic, rural and now metropolitan circumstances; on their own soil, as well as, unhappily and happily, among other peoples. And they are a people who, through-out all these experiences, have found a way to serve the Lord, their God.

The people of Israel are a people of hope. If they have anything to say to mankind in these difficult days, it is that we must not despair; that the Messiah will come; the Kingdom of God will be with us. To this faith and hope the people of Israel stand in steadfast testimony, today just as they have in the past.

JUDAISM: ORTHODOX, CONSERVATIVE AND REFORM

Dr. Michael Wyschogrod

Jewish Life: A Study in Diversity

To the Biblical interpreter, the 49th chapter of Genesis is something of an enigma. Jacob, the last of the three patriarchs, is about to die, and he gathers about him his 12 sons "so that I may tell you that which shall befall you in the end of days." To each of them he then addresses a sentence or two, poetic in form and somewhat mysterious in meaning, but which unmistakably indicates that he not only understands their individuality and uniqueness, but also the special role each of them is to play in the destiny of the Jewish people.

Ever since those ancient days, Jewish life has been a fascinating study in diversity: a collage of faces, activities, tempers, ideologies and cultures. Even the face of the Jew is diverse—sometimes swarthy and oriental, because Jews have participated in the cultures of Yemen and India; sometimes Nordic and blonde, because Jews have also been part of the cultures of Germany and the United States. For the same reason, Jewish prayer may be addressed to God in the high-pitched wail that reflects the tonality of the Middle East, or in the sometimes sad, sometimes joyful, melodies of the Hassidim that reflect the Slavic environment in which they developed.

If, at times, this diversity is bewildering even to the Jew himself, how much more it must be then to the interested non-Jew! One has only to visit synagogues to be struck at once with this diversity. In some, men pray with their heads covered and are separate from the women; in others, men pray with their heads uncovered and are permitted to sit together with women. Some other examples. For the Orthodox Jew, the Sabbath runs from sundown Friday to nightfall Saturday, and involves

---

Based on the original script delivered on closed-circuit television.

(among other things) abstention from travel, one's daily work, the use of electricity and cooking. In short, the Sabbath is a sacred day of rest to be spent in worship, study and family-togetherness. Reform Jews, on the other hand, are not obliged to abstain from the kind of work forbidden to the Orthodox, and the whole meaning of the Sabbath day is interpreted in a more liberal spirit. Furthermore, whereas Reform Jews will eat in the same restaurants that non-Jews frequent, the Orthodox Jew will only eat at home or in so-called *kosher* restaurants, *i.e.,* those which serve the kind of food that the Jewish dietary laws prescribe as permissible to be eaten.

To the American who is not a member of the Jewish faith, and who observes these and other differences, certain questions very naturally present themselves. For instance, how many different kinds of Judaism exist in this country? What is their significance? How did they come into being? To give a satisfactory answer, one must go back to past history.

Different Kinds of Judaism: Past History in the United States

Throughout medieval times the majority of Jews lived in Europe,[1] in most instances under conditions that tended to isolate them from their non-Jewish neighbors. In other words, they lived in ghettoes, as a result of which a way of life established itself which was dominant for a long time. With the Enlightenment, however, certain things changed. Jews were now admitted into the universities, as well as into other areas of national life. As more and more Jews entered the professions and began to make their lives in industry, politics, etc., the restrictions that the Law imposed on them, particularly in terms of the Sabbath and of the dietary laws, became increasingly difficult to observe. The result was that many erstwhile Orthodox Jews gradually began to abandon the practice of these particular aspects of Judaism without, however, feeling that in so doing they had thereby separated themselves from the rest of the Jewish people. In time, they developed synagogues whose ritual was somewhat different, and adopted a position in which the observance of the Sabbath and of the dietary laws was no longer considered to be as crucial as it had been earlier. In short, they became Reform Jews.

American Reform Judaism: The Pittsburgh Platform (1885)

In our country, of course, this process developed at an even more rapid rate. The Jews who came here adapted very quickly to the open-

---

1. There were also a considerable number of Jews living in North Africa, but these remained relatively unaffected by change, and so are not discussed here.

ended society that was the United States. As a result, many congregations grew up that followed Reform rituals. Thus, in 1885, 19 American Rabbis who shared this Reform orientation met in Pittsburgh, under the chairmanship of the man most prominently identified with Reform Judaism in the United States—Isaac M. Wise. There they adopted a manifesto that came to be known as "The Pittsburgh Platform" which, with some significant modifications, is still relevant to American Reform Judaism. Among other things, it had the following to say:

> We recognize in every religion an attempt to grasp the infinite . . . the consciousness of the in-dwelling of God in man. We hold that Judaism presents the highest conception of the 'God idea' as taught in our Holy Scriptures and developed and spiritualized by Jewish teachers in accordance with the moral and philosophical progress of their respective ages. We recognize, in the Mosaic Legislation, the system of training the Jewish People for its mission during its national life in Palestine. (However,) today we accept as binding only the moral laws and maintain only such ceremonies as elevate and sanctify our lives; but reject all such as are not adapted to the views and habits of modern civilization. We hold that all such Mosaic and Rabbinical Laws that regulate diet, priestly purity in dress, (etc.) originated in ages and under the influence of ideas altogether foreign to our present mental and spiritual state. They fail to impress the modern Jew with a spirit of priestly holiness. Their observance in our days is apt rather to obstruct than to further modern spiritual elevation. We recognize, in the modern era of universal culture of heart and intellect, the approaching of the realization of Israel's great Messianic hope and the establishment of the kingdom of truth, justice and peace among all men. We consider ourselves no longer a nation but a religious community, and, therefore, expect neither a return to Palestine, nor a sacrificial worship out of the Sons of Aaron, or the restoration of any of the laws concerning the Jewish State.

> In full accordance with this spirit of Mosaic Legislation which strives to regulate the relation between rich and poor, we deem it our duty to participate in the great task of modern times; to solve, on the basis of justice and righteousness, the problems presented by the contrasts and evils of the present organization of society.

In the very last sentence, we find expressed the social consciousness of American Reform Judaism that has remained a part of it from the time of the "Pittsburgh Platform" to this very day. Thus we see the emphasis placed on social justice, on concern for the poor, on concern for those whose opportunities were not the same as those who succeeded. This emphasis still exists. At the same time, however, there are elements in the "Pittsburgh Platform" that most American rabbis would no longer accept today. Among these, for example, is the statement that we no longer expect a return to Palestine. The reason for this change is that, while in the 19th and the early part of the 20th century, much of Reform Judaism was anti-Zionist, this is no longer the case. And I think it is also fair to add that American Reform Judaism has returned, to some extent at least, to a position which gives increased significance to ritual (in the "Pittsburgh Platform," ritual did not always fully receive its due).

The Conservative School: Alexander Kohut (1885)

At the same time that the "Pittsburgh Platform" was being formulated, it should not be thought that the other branches of Judaism were standing silently by. There were those who felt Reform Judaism had gone too far, giving up too much of what was germane and essential to Judaism. This group, which may be called the "Historical School" (since it was given to thinking largely in terms of Jewish historical experience) has, in the 20th century, come to be known as the "Conservative School."

The "Conservative School" developed largely as a result of a reaction by certain Jews to the Reform platform outlined above. In his first address (1885) from the pulpit of Congregation Ahavath Chesed in New York City, Alexander Kohut, a scholar and leader of Hungarian Jewry, laid down the following principles that were to guide the Conservative Movement for many years to come:

> The chain of Tradition continued unbroken from Moses down to the latest times. On this Tradition rests our Faith which Moses first received from God on Sinai. On this foundation rests Mosaic Rabbinical Judaism today. And on this foundation we take our stand. The teaching of the Ancients we must make our starting point, but we must not lose sight of what is needed in every generation. Let's now revert to the question raised at the outset. Is Judaism definitely closed for all time, or is it capable of, and in need of, continuous development? I answer both 'yes' and 'no'. I answer 'yes' because religion has been given to man, as it is the duty of man to grow in perfection as long as he lives. He must modify

the forms which yield him religious satisfaction in accordance with the spirit of the times. I answer 'no' insofar as it concerns the word of God which cannot be imperfect. You Israelites, imperfect as you are, strive to perfect yourself in the image of your perfect God. Hold in honor His unchangeable law, and let it be your earnest task to put new life into the outward form of our religion. Our religious guide is the Torah, the Law of Moses, interpreted and applied in the light of Tradition. But inasmuch as individual opinion cannot be valid for the whole community, it behooves individuals and communities to appoint only recognized authorities as teachers. Such men, that is to say, as acknowledge belief in authority and who, at the same time, with comprehension and tact are willing to consider what may be permitted in view of the exigencies of the times, and what may be discarded without changing the nature and character of the foundations of the Faith.

Here we have in outline form the themes of Conservative Judaism that have remained essentially unchanged to our day. To Alexander Kohut and to most Conservative thinkers, there are those elements in the Torah, in the word of God and in the rabbinic tradition, which cannot, and must not, be changed. On the other hand, there are also certain elements which, they feel, can and must be changed. At the same time, the leaders of this movement were very insistent that the changes deemed proper and necessary be made not by the man in the street who finds himself under the exigencies of day-to-day life as he tries to adapt himself to the demands of the culture around him; but, rather, that these changes be made by those who were properly steeped in biblical and rabbinic literature, so that Judaism might continue the tradition of following the lead of the scholar and the rabbi. The delicate balance between change, on the one hand, and permanence, on the other, is one of the guiding motifs of Conservative Judaism, which can be seen to fall, then, somewhere between the positions of Reform and Orthodox.

American Orthodoxy (1898)

Orthodoxy in the United States is that branch of Judaism which has retained the largest degree of identification with the rabbinic Judaism of the Talmudic and Medieval Periods. To the Orthodox Jew, Judaism and its interpretation and application in the rabbinic text is divine. It is the word of God and *cannot* be changed. It may be interpreted, but only within the framework of the Law. This is the crucial concept that had guided and continues to guide Jewish Orthodoxy.

It took American Orthodoxy some years to adapt itself and make itself heard, because the first Orthodox immigrants to this country (who were from Eastern Europe) arrived later than other immigrants, and it therefore took some time for these people not only to learn English, but to learn to think in American terms. For these reasons, the Orthodox Jewish Congregational Union did not come into being until 1898, at which time it set down the following basic principles:

> We believe in the divine revelation of the Bible. And we declare that the Prophets in no way discountenanced ceremonial duties but only condemned the personal life of those who observed ceremonial Law but disregarded the morals. Ceremonial Law is not optative, it is obligative. We affirm our adherence to the acknowledged codes of our Rabbis and the 13 principles of Maimonides. We believe . . . that we are to be united with our brethren of alien faiths in all that devolves upon men as citizens; but that religiously, i.e., in rights, ceremonies, ideals and doctrines, we are separate and must remain separate in accordance with the divine declaration, 'I have separated you from the nations, to be mine.' And further, to prevent misunderstanding concerning Judaism, we reaffirm our belief in the coming of the Messiah, and we protest against the admission of proselytes into the fold of Judaism without circumcision and immersion. We protest against the idea that we are merely a religious sect and maintain that we are a nation, though temporarily without a national home. Furthermore, that the restoration to Zion is the legitimate aspiration of scattered Israel, in no way conflicting with our loyalty to the land in which we dwell, or may dwell, at any time.

There are many Orthodox Jews today who are active in all the trades and professions of this country and who, at the same time, obey very carefully the laws that have bound Judaism for many years. To the outside observer, this sometimes may seem difficult to reconcile. However, to the Jew who feels that he is fulfilling the word of God with love, the experience is one that draws him even closer to his God.

The Secular Jew

Finally, we have a type of Jew who is perhaps the most perplexing of all to the non-Jew—the secular Jew. On the face of it, this can seem like a contradiction in terms. Isn't Judaism a religion? And, if it is, what sense does it make to speak of a "secular Jew"? To understand this, one must approach the problem theologically. Judaism is the covenant of the Jewish people with God; the Jewish people is the seed of Abraham. It follows, therefore, that no matter what the ideology or belief of any given Jew may be, so long as he is a descendant of Abraham, he remains in this covenantal relationship with God. The secular Jew is not a contradiction in terms. He may have an ideology, which from the point of view of the believing Jew is erroneous, but that in no way detracts from his being a Jew. Thus there exist, in this country as well as in Europe, great numbers of Jews whose allegiance to the Jewish people is profound, who helped develop Jewish culture, yet who, ideologically, are secularists.

Significance of the Diversity and Division

What then is the significance of the divisions in contemporary Judaism that we have been discussing? Are these merely surface phenomena which leave the unity of the Jewish people basically unimpaired? Or would it be more accurate to say that Judaism is no longer a unified religion, and that what we have here, in effect, are different religions whose points of divergence will continue to increase with the passage of time? From my own point of view, both of these alternatives miss the mark. Just as one must be careful never to underestimate the importance of these differences, so one must be equally careful not to overestimate them. Certainly the differences in theology and practice that have been discussed are not minor. Whether a Jew is duty-bound to obey a law that's understood as coming from God and which covers what he eats as well as how he treats the poor, which is the Orthodox point of view; or whether the ethical portions of the Torah retain primacy, thus permitting the modern Jew to disregard those ritual commandments he considers outdated, which is the point of view of Reform Judaism and many segments of Conservative Judaism—this question is one that no thinking person can overlook. The fact that today there is profound disagreement among Jews as to the correct answer to this question (and others like it) is clear testimony to its importance. But to conclude that, because of this disagreement, the unity of the Jewish people has therefore been severed once and for all would perhaps be even more of an error.

The Israeli Jew: A New Breed?

In a recent book by Georges Friedmann, a French Jewish sociologist, the point is argued that the new generation born and raised in Israel is no longer Jewish; that, instead, they are Israelis who, being a new breed, have no real connection with the Jews of the Diaspora. "If," says Friedmann, "there is a Holy Place to which they are indifferent, it is surely the Wailing Wall—the symbol of a past, all traces of which in their view should be obliterated."

These words were written before the events of June, 1967, which made the Wailing Wall once again accessible to the Jews. What happened then? Well, as if to belie the validity of Friedmann's thesis, on the very first day that the general public was permitted to visit the Wall, hundreds of thousands of Jews streamed by it—Orthodox and non-Orthodox, European and African, the young and the old, men as well as women. Ever since then, this Wall, the only remaining fragment of the Temple that was destroyed in 70 A.D., has become once again a symbol of the indestructible unity of the Jewish people.

Summary and Conclusions

However serious the theological differences may be, however passionately they have been argued in the past and will continue to be argued for some time to come, the Jewish people are rediscovering (if they ever forgot) that so long as there are those for whom compassion and tolerance for one's fellow-man represent an intolerable intrusion into the so-called natural order of things, so long too will the Jewish people have to be prepared for what happened to them during the Holocaust to happen again. In Auschwitz and Dachau, no one asked the Jew whether he was Orthodox or Reform, whether he was secular or believing. Irrespective of such distinctions, real though they are, they were all put to death in the greatest mass murder in human history.

To the extent that the Messianic faith is at the heart of Jewish faith, to that same extent must the present divisions in the House of Israel be viewed as only temporary: as divisions to be overcome in the fullness of redeemed time.

THE LIFE CYCLE OF THE JEWS
(Torah, Marriage, Good Deeds)

Rabbi Jules Harlow

Introduction

In the creation of a new life there are three partners: God, and a man and a woman. Thus begins an ancient rabbinic statement dealing with the formation of the embryo. New life gives birth to much more than an infant. In view of the hopes and possibilities, what do you say to new parents? Congratulations, of course. But this expression is appropriate on many other occasions as well. There is a Hebrew phrase, however, which is especially appropriate to new life, and many Jews still use it in writing or speaking to new parents: "May you raise your child to a life blessed with Torah, marriage and good deeds." This wish for a specific kind of fulfillment is taken from the ritual that formally marks a Jewish infant's entry into the world.

Before presenting this phrase in its ritual context, let me amplify the individual terms. Torah technically refers to the Pentateuch, the first five books of the Bible. It can also refer to the handwritten parchment scroll containing these books kept in the synagogue and read from during services. It is likewise used in a larger context to refer to the study of Jewish texts and sources, in which one finds an ever changing emphasis and modification. Used in this last sense, Torah (in the words of Dr. Louis Ginzberg) is "the aggregate of all Jewish teaching." The study and perpetuation of this teaching is a cardinal principle of Jewish life and tradition.

Based on the original script delivered on closed-circuit television.

Marriage, as well as the family and home which it produces, is another crucial concern. The statement in the book of Genesis that "it is not good for man to be alone," is expanded upon in a rabbinic comment presenting the normative Jewish view that a man who lives without a wife lives without joy, without blessing, and without peace. A considerable portion of the Talmud is devoted to discussions and decisions on various aspects of the husband-wife relationship. Two of the Ten Commandments reflect God's concern for maintaining the sanctity of the marriage bond.

Good deeds are a crucial part of Jewish tradition, because Judaism does not direct man to be good in general. In Leo Baeck's words, "Judaism must not be a mere internalized experience, even of the most intense kind. . . . In the pious deed is the sustaining foundation of the confession of faith." In fact, charity in action is a much higher ideal than clarity in thought. A normative rabbinic view deems theory great when and because it leads to practice. This emphasis upon actual deeds is reflected in the statement of an ancient rabbi that there are times when a man must act as if there were no God. When asked to explain himself, the rabbi replied with the following example: If a poor man asks you for help, do not tell him to pray for it, do not offer your own prayer; rather, you must act as if there were no God, as if the man will not be helped unless *you* help him.

Birth

A child is born naked of deeds, and is thus neither good nor evil. According to an ancient rabbinic legend, the qualities of each person are decreed in the Heaven of Heavens before he is born. There and then everything is decided, except for one thing: whether the child to be born will develop into someone who is bad or someone who is good. This unfolds with life itself, reflected in the deeds each person performs. And the constant hope of the community of Israel is that each life will be one of fulfillment through Torah, marriage and good deeds.

Life begins with the first breath. Nonetheless, the thirtieth day of life is held to be especially significant, in that it introduces a quality of permanence into each life. Thus, if a child dies before its thirtieth day, the ordinary rites of mourning are not observed.

During the first week after the birth of a girl, the father will be honored at a synagogue service (usually on the Sabbath), by being one of those called upon to recite the benedictions of the Torah when it is read. Then the rabbi or some other officiant will recite a prayer asking that He who blessed our ancestors Abraham, Isaac, Jacob, Sarah, Rebecca, Rachel and Leah bless the mother and her newborn daughter, whose Hebrew name is then declared. The prayer ends with the hope for Torah, marriage and good deeds in the child's life.

Brit and Circumcision

A boy child is formally named as part of the ritual known as *bris,* or *brit,* circumcision. (At this point, a comment on the general subject of ritual is perhaps necessary. There is a variety of ritual observance in the Jewish community. The rituals which I refer to here are considered mandatory by the Orthodox and Conservative communities. Some of them are so considered by the Reform as well, though many others, stemming from ancient rabbinic tradition, are not to held to be obligatory. It should also be pointed out that there is a certain portion of the Jewish community who choose to observe none of the ritual practices or customs.)

The translation of *bris,* or *brit,* as circumcision is misleading. Circumcision indeed takes place, but the significance of the ceremony is contained in the literal meaning of the Hebrew word—covenant. Ever since Abraham, this sign of the covenant that God made with him has been sealed in the flesh during the ritual which takes place on the eighth day of a boy's life. This ritual grew out of the biblical injunction in Genesis first addressed to Abraham: "Throughout your generations, every male among you shall be circumcised when he is eight days old." However, if the child's health may be endangered by the circumcision, the ceremony must be postponed. The principle involved here is one which was frequently affirmed by the ancient rabbis. Expounding upon a verse in Leviticus, they declared that laws were given so that men should live by them, not die by them.

It is the father's obligation to bring his child into the covenant, and it is he who arranges for a ritual circumciser, or *mohel,* to carry it out. The *mohel* must have knowledge of the surgery required, as well as knowledge of Jewish law. After the circumcision, all present say: "As he has entered the covenant of Abraham, so may he attain the blessings of Torah, marriage and good deeds." (This phrase, incidentally, is also contained in the prayer which concludes the ceremony, and in which the infant is given a name.)

In giving boys and girls their Hebrew names, most often the name chosen is that of a relative no longer living whose memory is thus perpetuated. Each child bears a given name together with that of his or her father: for example, Isaac son of Abraham.

Since, in terms of Jewish tradition, a male convert to Judaism is

considered as though he were new-born and therefore has status equal
to that of a Jew at birth, he too is expected to fulfill the obligation of
ritual circumcision. In addition, both male and female converts must
undergo ritual immersion as part of the requirements for religious conversion. The convert is subsequently known in Hebrew as the son, or
daughter, of Abraham.

Redeeming of the First-born Male

If a Jewish male baby is the first-born of his mother, then his father
has an additional obligation: to redeem him, so to speak. This ritual
has its source in the book of Exodus, in which every first-born of the
womb, whether man or beast, is considered to belong to the Lord. In
biblical times the first-born in each family assisted the priests in worship.
Later, when this vocation was transferred to members of the clan known
as Levites, it was decreed that every father release (or "redeem") his
first-born son from the duties which would originally have been incum-
bent upon him. This practice continues to be carried out to the present
day. Thus, on the thirtieth day of the infant's life, the father opts to
redeem his son rather than give him to the *kohen* (one who descends
geneologically from the ancient priestly families), and gives the latter
five silver dollars, the equivalent of five biblical *shekalim*. As a rule, the
kohen donates this money to charity.

Bar Mitzvah (Bat Mitzvah)

The words often expressed that parents will raise their child to Torah
is more than a hope in Jewish tradition. It is an obligation of parents.
A passage in Deuteronomy, included in every synagogue service, declares that the Torah must be taught to one's children. Moses Maimonides, the famous medieval authority, while declaring that every Jew,
rich or poor, healthy or not, young or old, was obliged to study Torah,
considered such study especially crucial and precious in the case of
children. In a somewhat similar vein, the ancient rabbis declared that
the world is "poised upon the breath of school children."

Today the formal education of the Jewish child very often comes to
an abrupt end with the *bar mitzvah* ceremony which takes place when
a boy reaches the age of 13. This, of course, is a perversion of its original
purpose, since Jewish tradition conceives of study as an ongoing process
and obligation. Clear evidence of this can be seen in the way that the

rabbis of the Talmud interpreted a verse from the book of Joshua ("This book of the law, or Torah, shall not depart from your mouth"). According to their interpretation, the obligation to study the Torah is not like a debt which a man can discharge by paying a fixed amount; rather, it is an abiding duty from which no one has the authority to release himself.

What is the significance of becoming a *bar mitzvah?* Literally, the phrase means "son of the commandment." It signifies becoming a full-fledged member of the Jewish community who is obliged to fulfill God's commandments—*i.e.,* attaining one's religious majority. For example, after his thirteenth birthday a young man, now a *bar mitzvah,* is counted as one of the ten males who constitute a *minyan,* the required quorum for a public service of prayer. Thus he may participate with other adults at the reading of the Torah in the synagogue service. In fact, on the Sabbath following his thirteenth birthday, he is introduced to some of his new religious responsibilities by being asked in synagogue to chant the *haftorah,* or the prophetic portion of that day's service. Some young men will, in addition, read the appropriate section from the Torah scroll, or serve as cantor for the congregation. At thirteen, too, a young man first uses *tefillin,* ritual objects worn during morning prayer on all days other than the Sabbath and holidays. Two small leather boxes, each containing an inscribed parchment, are placed on the forehead and on the upper arm opposite the heart, and attached with leather straps. The parchment contains passages from the books of Deuteronomy and Exodus, declaring God's oneness and His dominion over all life, recalling the miracle of the Exodus from Egypt and affirming man's duty "to serve God with all one's soul and all one's heart and all one's mind."

It is traditional for the father of the *bar mitzvah* to invite family and friends to join in a subsequent celebration, just as it is traditional to celebrate the naming and circumcision of a child, or a wedding.

In recent times a parallel ceremony (*bat mitzvah*) has developed for a girl when she reaches the age of twelve. Her participation in the synagogue service varies, however, from community to community. She may read the prophetic portion, or otherwise participate in the service on Friday evening or Sabbath morning. In addition, a ceremony for boys as well as girls which is known as confirmation has developed in modern times. It takes place between the ages of fourteen and sixteen (usually upon the occasion of graduation from a congregational Sunday school), and is a way in which young people publicly affirm their commitment to Jewish faith.

Religious Education

It has been said that a city without pupils is doomed. The same is true of a religious tradition. Rabbi Judah the Prince expressed this idea in ancient times in his dictum that the study of schoolchildren could not be interrupted, even for the purposes of building the sacred Temple in Jerusalem. Today, Jewish communities consider at least a minimal education of their children in Hebrew and in religious studies to be an obligation which they must support; in fact, in a growing number of instances, education considerably beyond this minimum is involved. The latter is reflected in a number of different areas: in the afternoon Hebrew school, held after public school classes are dismissed; in the increasing numbers of Jewish day schools throughout the country; in Hebrew-speaking summer camps, as well as in camps where Jewish education in English is a major focus. A few communities likewise sponsor Hebrew Teachers Colleges, where students pursue their Hebrew and Judaica studies while working for their bachelor's degree at a local college.

Marriage

Ever since Adam, it has been basic to Jewish tradition that a man without a wife is not "complete." (Of course, marriage is completion for a woman as well.) The first commandment in the Bible is to "be fruitful and multiply," a commandment to be fulfilled by partners to a marriage; whereas the Talmud declares that, in the world to come, the first questions which will be asked of us are: "Did you deal honestly, in good faith? Did you have a set time for the study of Torah? Did you raise a family?" (This, incidentally, is yet another way of stating the primacy of the three categories of Torah, marriage and good deeds.)

On the Sabbath immediately preceding a wedding, the groom is honored in a synagogue during the Torah service. A prayer is recited on the couple's behalf, asking that they be privileged to fashion a Jewish home harboring love, harmony, peace and companionship, and that they be blessed with children reared in health and well-being, and devoted to Torah and good deeds.

During the wedding ceremony itself, bride and groom stand beneath a special canopy called a *hupah*. The *hupah* symbolizes the home, a shelter for those within it, and at the same time open to all (the *hupah* is itself open on all sides). In fact, the home is so significant in Jewish tradition that often the name of its symbol, *hupah,* is used as a synonym for wedding.

The modern Jewish wedding ceremony combines what formerly were two ceremonies—betrothal and marriage—though they are separated by many months. After the benedictions of betrothal, the couple share a cup of wine. As for the wedding ceremony, Jewish law prescribes that the ring used be a plain band, with no stones, so that no one should be embarrassed by an inability to provide an expensive ring. As the groom places the ring on his bride's finger, he recites in Hebrew the following ancient formula: "By this ring you are consecrated unto me according to the Law of Moses and the people of Israel." Consecration is so central to this ceremony that one of the names it bears in Hebrew is *kiddushin,* or sanctification. The wedding contract, *ketubah,* is then read. An ancient legal document, written in Aramaic, it sets forth a husband's obligations to honor and cherish his wife, to support her, and to provide for her should they become divorced or should she become a widow. In turn, the wife promises to fulfill her duties. (Throughout the years, clauses have sometimes been added, setting forth special terms for specific couples.) The *ketubah* is made out before the ceremony, and is signed by bride and groom as well as two witnesses who must not be related to either of them.

Seven benedictions are chanted by a cantor or rabbi which praise God as the Creator who fashioned man in His own image and who created man and woman so that together they might perpetuate life. The final benediction, which also reflects concern for the land of Israel and Jerusalem (so central to Jewish thought) reads:

> Praised are You, O Lord our God, King of the universe who created joy and gladness, bride and groom, mirth, song, delight and rejoicing, love and harmony, peace and companionship. O Lord our God, may there ever be heard in the cities of Judah and in the streets of Jerusalem voices of joy and gladness, voices of bride and groom, the jubilant voices of those joined in marriage under the bridal canopy, the voices of young people feasting and singing. Praised are You, O Lord who causes the groom to rejoice with his bride.

A second cup of wine is then shared by husband and wife.

At the conclusion of the ceremony the groom breaks a glass underfoot, thus symbolically mourning the destruction of the ancient Temple in Jerusalem. This gesture is also interpreted as a way of calling to mind the suffering of Jews persecuted in other areas of the world, and as a reminder that one's bond to the Jewish community at large obligates him to share its sorrows—even at moment of great personal joy.

Divorce

The sexual relationship of the married couple is held to be important not only for the purpose of procreation but for mutual pleasure. The sexual appetite is normal, and is to be satisfied and sanctified in marriage; willful refusal of sexual relations by either partner to a marriage is therefore grounds for divorce.

"When a home is broken by divorce, even the Temple altar sheds tears." So runs an ancient rabbinic statement. But, if living together becomes impossible for a husband and wife, divorce can be obtained. The relationship entered into by mutual consent and by religious ceremony is dissolved in the same way. The basis for this procedure is traced back to Deuteronomy. It is a complicated procedure affording opportunities to both partners for reflection and reconsideration. A writ of divorce, a stylized document, must be prepared by a scribe in the presence of witnesses. The document, or *get,* must be granted before either party to the marriage is free to marry again.

The Home

The home established by a married couple is considered to be a sanctuary in miniature (e.g., the table is an altar), as well as the scene of family joy each Sabbath and holidays. The Sabbath and holidays begin at sundown, and are ushered in shortly before when the woman of the household lights candles with an appropriate benediction. Sabbath and holiday meals begin when the head of the household recites *kiddush,* the sanctification of the holy day over a cup of wine. After a brief benediction praising God as creator of the fruit of the vine, the *kiddush* praises Him for having "sanctified us through His commandments . . . in love and in favor have You given us Your holy Sabbath, a reminder of Creation, and the first of the holy convocations, in remembrance of the exodus from Egypt . . . ." The *kiddush* on the Sabbath day contains the phrase, "God blessed the seventh day, and He hallowed it, because He rested thereon from all His work . . . ." Etymologically, the Hebrew word *kiddush* has overtones similar to *kiddushin,* the wedding ceremony of sanctification with which the Jewish home formally begins.

Special songs and hymns appropriate to the occasion are sung at the Sabbath and holiday table. It is also considered desirable to have a guest or guests at these meals. The guest may be a friend or relative, or a stranger met in synagogue. Hospitality plays a major role in Jewish home life, proudly tracing it roots back to the patriarch Abraham and the manner in which he is said to have received guests in his dwelling-place.

The dietary laws are another important aspect of Jewish home life, though they apply outside the home as well. The flesh of certain creatures (pigs and shellfish, for example) is not eaten at all; other animals, whose flesh is permitted to be eaten, must be slaughtered in such a way that a minimum of pain is caused and a maximum of blood drained away. There is also a strict separation of milk and meat products, and separate sets of dishes and utensils are maintained for each.

On the doorpost at the entrance to the home, and on doorways throughout the home, a *mezuzah* is attached, a small cylinder containing passages from the Torah. A central passage, from Deuteronomy, is the affirmation of faith: "Hear O Israel, the Lord is our God, the Lord is One." Upon entering and leaving the home, a person is thus constantly reminded of the quality of life he is bidden to maintain everywhere.

Caring for the Sick and Elderly

In the Song of Moses, recorded in Exodus, it is written: "This is my God and I shall glorify Him." A rabbi once asked, "How can any man glorify God?" Typically, he answered his own question, "By following God's ways, becoming His partner. As He is gracious and merciful, you be gracious and merciful. As He visits the sick, you visit the sick. As He comforts mourners, you comfort mourners. As He tends to the dead, you tend to the dead." This imitation of God applies to many occasions, joyous and sad. Thus it is a religious duty to help bride and groom rejoice on their wedding day, and to visit the sick, expressing compassion and concern. A set of laws governs this duty as well as all others including, in this particular case, such practical considerations as not burdening the sick with long visits.

Tending to the elderly is also a religious duty. I have previously spoken of the parents' obligations to children, but the child has obligations as well. These are expressed, for example, in the fifth of the ten commandments: "Honor your father and your mother." In the event, however, that an elderly person's family is for some reason not able to take care of him, the entire community takes the obligation upon itself. In fact, many Jewish communities maintain their own homes for the aged.

Death and Burial

There is a Hebrew phrase—*chesed shel emet*—which can loosely be translated as "loving-deeds done without the expectation of reward." The phrase is often applied to deeds performed for the dead or dying.

Most congregations or communities maintain a holy fellowship, *chevra kadisha,* whose members are devoted to assisting families visited by the angel of death. Their assistance is usually related to various ritual aspects, but their concern is expressed in other ways as well.

As life begins, so it ends—that is the cycle. In Jewish tradition, a final confession is prescribed for the dying. If the latter is unable to read or recite this confession, it may be done on his behalf. A Jew's last words consist of the traditional affirmation of faith—"Hear O Israel, the Lord is our God, the Lord is One"—words learned early as a child, words inscribed on the entrance to the home, words central to every prayer service.

Respect for the dead person requires burial as soon as possible. Dignity and simplicity are essential. The body is washed, ritually cleansed, clothed in plain linen shrouds and placed in a plain wooden coffin. The purpose here is both to discourage lavish funerals, too often beyond the means of the bereaved, and to emphasize the basic equality of all people, whom death visits without exception. Embalming is forbidden. Man is formed of dust, and to dust he shall return, a process which Jewish tradition feels should not be interfered with.

Attending the funeral and accompanying the dead to the cemetery is still another religious obligation. At the funeral, mourners in the immediate family tear an article of clothing as a symbol of their grief, though today many tear a black ribbon instead, which is attached to their clothing. They likewise recite a benediction (from a passage in Job) praising God as the righteous judge: "The Lord has given and the Lord has taken away; may the name of the Lord be praised." Funeral ceremonies are essentially simple, consisting of passages from the Bible and Rabbinic literature, a brief prayer and a brief eulogy.

At the cemetery, after the body is lowered into the grave, the prayer known as *kaddish* is recited by the children of the deceased. *Kaddish*—similar etymologically to the *kiddushin* of marriage and the *kiddush* of Sabbath and holidays—is another santification: in this case, of God. It is praise of God and a prayer for the institution of His kingdom on earth. Death is not mentioned in the *kaddish,* which is an act and a declaration of faith in the face of sorrow and loss. To emphasize the public nature of this declaration, tradition requires that it be recited in the presence of a *minyan,* or ten male adults—the minimum quorum for a public prayer service.

Kaddish is recited in synagogue services for eleven months after burial of a parent, and every year thereafter on the anniversary of the parent's death. It is also recited each year at the memorial services held on the Day of Atonement and on the three pilgrim festivals. In this sense, it serves as an instrument for binding one generation to another.

For seven days after the burial, the immediate family is confined to its home and visited by family, friends and members of the community. This is the period known as *shivah,* which means "seven." Services are held in the home, and *kaddish* is recited. It is customary, too, for food to be prepared for the mourners by others. A candle, symbolic of the soul, is lit during the entire week of *shivah* and at each anniversary thereafter.

To Jews, death ends the cycle, but death is not the end. The living confront death by perpetuating a centuries-old practice of sanctification and faith, reciting the mourner's *kaddish.* The ritual acts observed in mourning help to sanctify Israel as a people, as well as the life of each individual Jew. The attachment to holiness symbolized by these, as well as all other, ritual acts in the life of the Jew bespeaks and reflects his constant attempt to fulfill the Biblical injunction: Be holy, for I the Lord your God am holy.

Teachers' Guide to
JEWS and their RELIGION

INTRODUCTION

The basic resource material for this guide is to be found in Section I, which contains the full-length scripts of the seven original closed-circuit TV programs on "Jews and Their Religion." Teachers who are able to view these programs (now available on film) will benefit from the dramatic presentation of the lectures, as well as from the visual material that accompanies them. It should be remembered, however, that the present guide was prepared with the idea in mind that not all teachers will have access to the films, and it is for this reason especially that the lectures have been included in printed form.

The seven film scripts, each of them delivered by a scholar or a rabbi who is an authority on his subject, cover the following six topics: Who is the American Jew?; What is Judaism?; Aspects of Jewish Theology (2 parts); Jews and Their Worship; Judaism: Orthodox, Conservative, and Reform; The Life Cycle of a Jew. However, since even seven half-hour films can just skim the surface of a subject as broad as "Jews and Their Religion," this guide provides additional resource and bibliographical material. (One topic, for example, that was not covered by any of the film scripts is the Jewish calendar—i.e., the Sabbath and the holidays—and the guide, therefore, includes the necessary supplementary material.)

For convenience, as well as for organizational and conceptual purposes, the guide has been divided into four parts or sections, each of which covers one or more of the film scripts. They are:

I   The American Jew
II   What Jews Believe
III   Jewish Worship and the Jewish Year
IV   The Life of the Jew

This breakdown was arrived at, because it seemed to offer the widest possibilities for the teacher, depending on the time and resources available to him. Ideally, this entire series can be utilized as presented; if necessary, however, a meaningful unit of study can be created by the teacher from any one of the four sections.

Each section of the guide contains expository material that either amplifies or clarifies the subject at hand (with references, of course, to the lectures, suggested classroom activities and discussion topics, and a bibliography). One purpose of the expository material is to focus attention on the central elements of Jewish belief and practice. Another is to pinpoint specific topics surrounding which there is apt to be confusion and misunderstanding. All of us, after all, have our personal "understood" meanings for certain words and concepts which we no longer bother to think about, and which prevent us from understanding the connotation that someone else may attach to them.

In the study we are undertaking here, this is certainly the case. God, Covenant, Bible, Law, Pharisee, Messiah, Sin, Redemption, Israel, Jerusalem—these are but a few examples of words that Christians understand one way, Jews another. In fact, if one can state an overall aim for this study of Judaism, it might be "to clear the student's mind of all preconception and bias, so that he may come to understand the Jewish religion as a Jew understands it."

One of the difficulties inherent in trying to present a systematic picture of the Jewish religion is that Judaism is not a doctrinal religion; rather, it is a religion that has evolved—and is still evolving—over several thousand years, largely in response to the changing life circumstances of the people who call themselves Jews. True, there is a basic core of beliefs—about God and about themselves—that Jews in all ages and places have held and still hold in common. But the superstructure has undergone many alterations and accommodated to many variations —most of which have come in time to be considered acceptable, even desirable.

Because Judaism has to such a large degree grown in response to the history of the Jewish people, the student should have a fair grasp of that history. The script "What is Judaism?" provides a brief but instructive view, but the teacher will no doubt want to include books written on this subject in his own as well as his students' reading program so as to examine the questions in greater depth.

Another related area that is touched on in the guide is what Rev. Walter M. Abbott, S.J., has called "the terrible history of Christian-Jewish relations." Though this subject does not properly belong in a study limited to the Jewish religion, nonetheless it must at some point be placed on the agenda of the Catholic high school. The extent to which Jews have suffered at the hands of Christians is a fact not known by most Christians—and it is a fact that must be faced openly if the current dialogue is to prove meaningful and fruitful. (See General Reference Works: Flannery, E. H., *Anguish of the Jews: Twenty-three Centuries of Anti-Semitism.*)

Some word of explanation is called for regarding the inclusion of a section on the American Jews in material that is intended to deal solely with the Jewish religion. One reason for this was to provide both teacher and student with an easy and natural entry point to the overall study of Judaism. Christian students may know little or nothing about Judaism, but they almost certainly know and have met American Jews. In addition, this overview of the American Jewish community should enable the teacher to clarify for his class the very nature of Judaism: that it is a religion, to be sure, but that it is also the rich socio-cultural heritage of a diverse people that has shared a long history. The point is that Judaism encompasses people who accept its religious tenets—whether in traditional or modern form; people who may deny the beliefs, yet retain certain practices; and people who do neither, but identify themselves culturally and/or socially as Jews. It is most important, therefore, to understand that Judaism can contain this wide spectrum of belief, practice and commitment—while retaining its basic form and outline.

Inestimable assistance was given the writer of this guide by Brother Joseph Irwin, F.S.C., who was a true partner in this venture. His insights into the Catholic understanding of Jewish concepts were invaluable.

RUTH SELDIN

THE AMERICAN JEW

Aims and Objectives

1. To help the non-Jewish student grasp the diverse nature of the American Jewish community—its origins, beliefs, affiliations, life styles, etc.
2. To make clear the factors that unify Jews in general and the American Jew in particular.
3. To examine the history of Jews in this country, and their contributions to various areas of life.
4. To lead the Christian student to scrutinize his own attitudes toward Jews.
5. To evaluate the degree to which anti-Semitism is evidenced in the local community and elsewhere in the United States.
6. To inform the student about the major American Jewish organizations and their function.
7. To examine the attitudes of American Jews toward the State of Israel.
8. To consider the probable future in the U. S. A. of the Jewish community, as well as that of other ethnic and religious minorities.

Overview

Before looking into the system of beliefs and practices that we call *Judaism,* we are going to look very briefly at the American Jew himself.

As we already have indicated in the Introduction to this Guide, Judaism is a complex structure—it is a religion, to be sure, but it is a well-developed culture as well. What this means, exactly, might be formulated this way: it is possible to feel strongly Jewish, to identify with the Jewish heritage, and yet not be religiously observant. For non-Jews, this is often a puzzling or difficult thing to understand; therefore, it might be helpful to first consider the American Jew and to examine who and what he is, what he believes, what he identifies with.

There is a great deal of insight in the story that Dore Schary tells about Rabbi Morris Adler. (See "Who is the American Jew") Rabbi Adler found that his Christian colleagues were more at ease with him after he grew a beard. Because of the beard, apparently, the Christian clergymen identified the rabbi with Jesus, whom they knew about—and the rabbi, therefore, was no longer "strange."

What troubles and confuses many non-Jews is precisely the fact that the American Jew of the twentieth century is not a Palestinian Jew of the first century, nor is he the medieval figure of literature, lusting after Christian blood, who existed for so long in the non-Jewish imagination.

A close reading of Mr. Schary's script is strongly recommended. Almost none of the material needs any further explanation, but to summarize the portrait of the American Jew, as depicted by Mr. Schary, the following points should be stressed:

1) Some Jews consider themselves religious, others do not; almost all, however, identify as Jews, and may, if they choose, participate actively in cultural or communal aspects of Jewish life.

2) The State of Israel definitely plays a part in the thoughts and feelings of most American Jews; no matter what their religious position. Some Jews are ardent supporters of Israel, others feel less closely involved. But, almost no Jew is indifferent to Israel or to her fate.

3) American Jews are devoted and loyal citizens of the United States, and they see no conflict between their loyalty to this country and the help they give to their fellow Jews throughout the world. In fact, they believe that the American heritage and the Jewish heritage enrich one another, and they strive to blend both, creatively, in their own lives as well as the lives of their children.

In summing up the development of the Jewish community in the United States one finds:*

> . . . (that it) is deviating from the course which the other ethnic groups have followed in the process of integrating themselves into the larger American society. Those groups, in contradistinction to the settlers who built a new civilization on the basis of an old culture, have discarded their old cultures in order to adapt themselves to the new civilization dominated by the Anglo-Saxon elements. The greater the distance a group has covered on the road to adaptation, the farther it has moved away from its own ethnic moorings. The Jews have proved to be an exception to this rule, and herein lies their uniqueness as an ethnic community.

*The Jew Within American Society, C. Bezalel Sherman, Wayne State University, 1965, pp. 225-7.

Originally fragmented in their cultural views and communal activities, and subsequently achieving a high degree of acculturation in a short period of time, the Jews, had they fitted into the general patterns of integration, should have reached a state of near-dissolution as a community by the third generation. Instead the opposite has occurred, in contradiction to the history of the other European immigrant groups.

The contradiction consists in the growth and solidification of the Jewish community coming about partly *because of* American assimilatory trends and partly *in spite of* them. Inner forces of cohesion within the Jewish group have turned acculturation itself into an instrument to develop and to strengthen ethnic individuality. The persistent majority attitudes peculiar to American . . . resisted the complete assimilation even of those wavering Jews who may have actually desired to leave the Jewish fold. Utilitarianism, pragmatism and democracy have been transformed into factors of Jewish ethnic consolidation.

This consolidation has been reinforced by the condition of the Jewish people throughout the world. In this respect, too, the Jews have deviated from the main highway of adaptation. Not only was concern for Jews persecuted abroad a powerful stimulus for ethnic cohesion here, but the emergence of the State of Israel has so far had the effect of increasing rather than lessening the sense of belongingness among American Jews.

The disappearance of the Jews as a separate group is not in sight as long as prevailing social conditions in the United States and the existent world situation of the Jewish people continue. In this sense, the Jews bear a greater similarity to the colored races—the Negroes, Chinese, Japanese, Indians, and others whose status is that of castes or quasi-castes—than to the other immigrant groups that came here from Europe. But this particular status has only in part been imposed upon the Jews by the tyranny of the majority. It is also in no small measure the result of a free choice by the Jews themselves. For this reason, they may be expected to continue as a distinct ethnic group—on the level of spiritual uniqueness, religious separateness, ethnic consolidation and communal solidarity, but not in a political sense. They can have no prospective status other than that of a minority, albeit not as a discriminated against a minority as the Negroes. Within the limits in which they can function as a community, there is yet room for expansion and progress.

It is not the task of this study to decide whether or not it is good for the Jews that in time they will remain perhaps the sole exception among white ethnic groups; for the country as a whole it is certainly no disadvantage. For it is only as a community that the Jews can best and most effectively inject their tone into the American symphony—and thus help bridge the chasm between culture and civilization. For the Jews themselves this is the fact: they exist as a separate ethnic group and will remain so in the foreseeable future. Thus, their own welfare and the best interests of the United States require that they infuse their ethnic individuality with as much positive content as possible and that they bear their ethnic identity with pride. The difference between them and a caste or quasi-caste is the voluntarism with which they approach their separateness. If they were to retain their ethnic identity solely because the majority refuses to absorb them, then their existence would be marked by all the frustrations and bitterness that naturally accompany externally imposed separateness, and their spirit would bear the imprint of the entire misfortune of marginality. If, on the other hand, their group identity is founded on their will to live and to enrich America with whatever creative originality they possess—then they will be able to make of their exceptional status a joy to themselves and a blessing for the United States."

Suggested Classroom Activities and Discussion Topics

This material is suitable for use—with occasional modification—by Catholic, Protestant and Jewish groups.

1. What is Judaism? What is a Jew? Discuss these questions without benefit of research or lecture, trying to arrive at working definitions of the terms "Jew" and "Judaism." A member of the class should be chosen to write down the agreed-upon definitions, and to make note of any questions that arise during the discussion. Then, after the class has concluded its study of Judaism, return to these definitions and questions to see whether the original definitions are still acceptable, and if the questions have been answered or are more readily answerable.

2. Show the class a film or filmstrip about immigration to this country —the origins and contributions of settlers from many lands (i.e., that we are a nation of immigrants). (See "Additional Resources.")

3. Why did Jews come to this country? Where did they come from? What did they find? The Lower East Side of New York City at the turn of the century was the first home of the grandparents and great-grandparents of most of today's Jewish teenagers. Have a committee read and report on any or all of the following books: Hutchins Hapgood's *The Spirit of the Ghetto* (1902) and *Types from City Streets* (1910); Jacob A. Riis's *How the Other Half Lives* (1890), *The Children of the Poor* (1892), and *The Battle with the Slums* (1902); and Lincoln Steffens' *Autobiography*. Note that the preceding books are all by non-Jewish writers, whereas the titles that follow are by Jewish writers—Abraham Cahan's *The Rise of David Levinsky* (1917), Henry Roth's *Call It Sleep* (1934), Alfred Kazin's *A Walker in the City* (1951), and Maurice Hindus' *The Old East Side* (1969).

4. Have students write and tell stories about the experiences of their own immigrant forbears. Compare with those of Jewish immigrants. What problems did all share? What were their fears, their hopes? What did they find on coming to the "Golden Land"? If students can secure "first person" accounts, fine; otherwise the teacher may suggest appropriate reading matter (see question #3 and the bibliography) for this section.

5. The waves of Jewish immigration to this country are divided into three periods: 1654-1800; 1820-1880; 1882-1920. Assign students to read and report on the origins of these three groups, the impetus for their coming, where they settled in the U. S., their occupations, etc. The reports should include background material on the overall American scene in each period (e.g., Who else came and why?). Three books that can be particularly useful in this regard are: *A Nation of Immigrants* by John F. Kennedy, Harper & Row (revised edition, 1964), *Portal to America: The Lower East Side 1870-1925* by Allon Schoener, Holt, Rinehart and Winston (1967), *The Uprooted* by Oscar Handlin, Atlantic Monthly Press (1951).

6. Organize an informal census of Jews in the neighborhood to find out when they or their ancestors came to the U.S.A., from where, why they came, where all family members have since settled, etc.

The final compilation of data should constitute an interesting and informative picture of American Jews.

7. For more advanced students the census project might be expanded to include information about membership in organizations, synagogues, lodges, etc., making sure that students find out what the purposes of the organizations are. A few students may be assigned to secure information from the national offices of Jewish organizations (consult the *American Jewish Year Book*).

8. Though Jews are a small minority in this country (about six million), they are influential in a number of areas of American life. This may be a fruitful subject for research, thought and discussion. In what fields are Jews especially prominent? What characteristics may have helped bring this about? In what fields are Jews little active? Why? To what extent is anti-Jewish discrimination responsible for the occupational distribution of Jews?

9. Though instances of overt anti-Semitism are rare in this country, more subtle forms of anti-Jewish discrimination still exist and a national study has just revealed that two-thirds of the American population harbor some degree of anti-Semitic prejudice. Have students discuss: anti-Jewish attitudes and actions that they personally have witnessed or know about; their own attitudes to Jews and the attitudes of their families; the effect on their thinking of the statement on the Jews by the Vatican II Council.

10. We have witnessed in the last couple of years an increased tension between blacks and Jews in large cities. Discuss the following: to what extent this tension exists; its probable causes; reactions of Christian whites to black-Jewish relations; the role of Jews in civil rights work; possible "solutions" to the problem.

11. For schools located in New York City, an interesting activity might be a trip to any or all of the following places of interest: Lower East Side (Jewish bookstores, food stores); Spanish-Portuguese Synagogue (Congregation Shearith Israel); Temple Emanuel; House of Living Judaism; ILGWU Headquarters; Jewish Museum; Jewish Theological Seminary; Yeshiva University. (Other cities like Boston, Philadelphia, Charleston, Chicago, Detroit, St. Louis, Los Angeles, San Francisco, etc., also have their share of places. For guidance, the teacher may consult *The Jewish Tourist's Guide to the U.S.* by B. Postal.)

12. A study of Jewish involvement in the labor union movement in this country could very well focus on the garment industry, one of New York's largest industries, and on the ILGWU, which has always been a leader in the area of social legislation as well as in the improvement of working conditions. What is there in the Jewish religion and/or in the historical experience of Jews that has bred this special concern?

13. In Dore Schary's presentation, he states that "The Jewish family retains an undiminished sense of loyalty and cohesiveness." Have students discuss whether or not this statement is accurate, in terms of their own experience; the reasons why it was certainly true in the past and what factors influence Jewish family life at present. Students should also be asked to compare and contrast family life among varying ethnic groups.

14. If possible, have the class make a firsthand study of a local community institution that was established by Jews: a YMHA, a hospital, settlement house, home for the aged or infirm, orphanage, etc. (The Federation of Jewish Philanthropies in New York is a good source for information.) Students should find out when the institutions were established, by whom, and for what reasons; to what extent they are now supported by Jews, and how much their services are used by Jews and non-Jews.

15. In every large city, Catholics, Protestants and Jews support their own social, health and welfare agencies. Should these agencies be used exclusively by members of the sponsoring denomination or group? What factors should determine how these agencies are to be utilized and by whom? This discussion topic can be related to the above activity.

16. Many young Jews are torn between what may be conflicting desires: to be involved in their own Jewish culture and faith, and to be fully integrated in the larger Christian or secular society. Have students discuss these questions: Do you think a Jewish boy or girl should "do his own thing" and lead a Jewish way of life? Can a Jew who identifies positively with Judaism still be part of American culture, have non-Jewish friends, etc.? Does this same conflict exist for Catholic teenagers? For black teenagers? For white Protestant teenagers? What is cultural pluralism?

17. Instances of overt anti-Semitism are rare in this country, but anti-

Jewish prejudice in various forms still exists. To help students discuss openly their own attitudes toward Jews—positive as well as negative—have students list their own questions and attitudes about Jews and Judaism. After the lists are collected, copy the salient questions and comments on the blackboard and discuss. Incidentally, this same technique can be used when learning about other groups.

18. In Dore Schary's script, he refers to the biblical injunction on caring for the sick and aged, etc. In fact, St. Paul, during his missionary journies to Asia Minor, never lost sense of this rabbinic value, as he continually stressed the "collection" for poor Christians in Judea (See Acts 11:29 or Gal. 2:10). Discuss.

19. Do you find Jews to be radical, liberal, conservative or reactionary on the political spectrum? Is there such a thing as the Jewish vote? What connection, if any, is there between a Jew's political beliefs and habits and the religious beliefs of Judaism?

20. Can we speak of the Jewish American in the exact same way we speak of the Catholic American? Yes or no, and why?

Bibliography

The following is a selected listing of books and other resource material, mostly from Jewish sources, that will prove helpful in a study of the American Jew. For a more comprehensive bibliography, the teacher may wish to send for *A Bibliography on Judaism and Jewish-Christian Relations,* published by the Anti-Defamation League of B'nai B'rith, 315 Lexington Ave., New York, N.Y. 10016 (price $1.00).

The teacher will also find relevant listings in the other bibliographies in this guide.

    1—Indicates books suggested for the average high-school student.
    2—Indicates books suggested for the superior high-school student.
    3—Indicates books suggested for the average teacher.
    4—Indicates books suggested for further reading.

2   Eisenberg, A., editor. *The Golden Land.* New York: Thomas Yoseloff, 1964.

     Dozens of writers are represented in this anthology of essays, fiction and poetry. Eighty-five selections intended to give a literary portrait of American Jewry from 1654 to the present.

3 Glazer, N. *American Judaism.* Chicago: University of Chicago Press, 1957 (paperback.)

A socio-historical analysis of the American Jewish community and its roots in Europe.

2 Glazer, N. and Moynihan, P. *Beyond the Melting Pot: The Negroes, Puerto Ricans, Jews, Italians and Irish of New York City.* Cambridge: M.I.T. Press (paperback).

A highly-regarded sociological study of the characteristics, contributions and problems of the major immigrant groups that settled in New York. Very readable.

1 Grayzel, S. *A History of the Contemporary Jews.* New York: Atheneum, 1969 (paperback).

A brief, easy-to-read account of modern Jewish history (from 1900 onward). Somewhat prone to over-generalization.

4 Grinstein, H. B. *Rise of the Jewish Community of New York.* Philadelphia: Jewish Publication Society, 1945.

The most complete account of Jewish history in New York; scholarly and not for the casual reader.

2 Handlin, O. *Adventure in Freedom: 300 Years of Jewish Life in America.* New York: McGraw-Hill, 1954.

An interpretation and "retrospective stocktaking" of American Jewish history through 1954.

2 Hapgood, H. *The Spirit of the Ghetto: Studies of the Jewish Quarter of New York.* New York: Schocken 1965 (paperback).

A remarkable work written at the turn of the century by a sensitive and perceptive non-Jew. Harry Golden provides preface and running commentary. There are also over 50 drawings by the sculptor, Jacob Epstein.

3 Hartstein, J. I., editor. *The Jews in American History.* New York: ADL, 1958.

A simple, well-organized and valuable resource book for teachers which also includes a section on the Jewish religion, a short survey of Jewish history and many resource materials.

3 Herberg, W. *Protestant, Catholic, Jew: An Essay in American Religious Sociology.* Garden City: Doubleday, 1960. (Also in paperback.)

A key study of the effects of religious pluralism on the three major American religious groups. This important work has had a major impact on leaders of the various religious hierarchies.

2   Hindus, M., editor. *The Old East Side: An Anthology*. Philadelphia: Jewish Publication Society, 1969.
>   An excellent collection of fact and fiction on what for a long time was the major American Jewish "ghetto."

2   Rosenberg, S. *The Search for Jewish Identity in America*. Garden City: Doubleday, 1965.
>   A popular and well-organized exposition of the history of the American Jewish community.

Pamphlets

The following pamphlets, which are relevant to the subject of the American Jew, are published by the Anti-Defamation League. To order, write c/o Publications Department.

Ackerman, W. L. *Jewish Religious Education*. 19 pp. 25 cents.
>   Traces the history of Jewish religious education from biblical times to present-day America.

ADL Staff. *The Jewish Family*. 16 pp. 25 cents.
>   Evaluates the popular image of the Jewish family, the relationship between the Jewish religion and the Jewish home, the Jewish attitude toward marriage, divorce, juvenile delinquency and alcoholism.

Handlin, O. *American Jews: Their Story*. 48 pp. 35 cents.
>   A brief illustrated history of Jewish life in America from 1654 to the present. Historical documents, photographs, Teacher Guide.

Fiction for Young People.

Abrahams, R. D. *The Commodore: The Adventurous Life of Uriah P. Levy*. Philadelphia: Jewish Publication Society, 1954.
>   About a Jewish naval hero of the War of 1812.

Blanford, B. W. *Off the Capes of Delaware*. New York: Union of American Hebrew Congregations, 1950.
>   Stories of American Jewish heroes.

Cohen, F. C. *Portrait of Deborah*. New York: Julian Messner, 1961
>   About a Jewish high-school senior and her relationship with a non-Jewish boy.

Emery, A. *Dinny Gordon: Freshman*. Philadelphia: Macrae Smith, 1964.
>   The reactions of a Protestant group to the arrival of a Jewish brother and sister in their community.

Hobart, L. *Strangers Among Us*. New York: Funk and Wagnalls, 1957.
A Jewish girl and her family move to a non-Jewish Midwestern town.

Lewiton, M. *Rachel and Herman*. New York: Franklin Watts, 1966.
The story of an immigrant family of the 1900's.

Mudra, M. *Look Beyond Tomorrow*. New York: Dutton, 1957.
A Jewish boy tries to hide his identity—then thinks better of it.

Biographies for Young People.

Alexander, L. *The Flagship Hope: Aaron Lopez*. Philadelphia: Jewish Publication Society, 1960.
A Portuguese Marrano who became a leading Jew in colonial America.

Apsler, A. *Northwest Pioneer: The Story of Louis Fleischner*. Philadelphia: Jewish Publication Society, 1960.
An immigrant Jew in the 1800's goes West.

Berkman, T. *Cast a Giant Shadow: The Story of Mickey Marcus*. Philadelphia: Jewish Publication Society.
A powerful biography of the West Point soldier who gave up his life while fighting to save Jerusalem during Israel's War of Independence. Originally an adult book which was subsequently made into a movie, it is now available in an edition for a younger age.

Fast, H. *Haym Salomon: Son of Liberty*. New York: Messner, 1941.
A leading financier of the Revolutionary War.

Kuhn, L. H. *The World of Jo Davidson*. Philadelphia: Jewish Publication Society, 1958.
A great sculptor who started life on the Lower East Side of New York.

Merriam, E. *The Voice of Liberty: The Story of Emma Lazarus*. Philadelphia: Jewish Publication Society, 1959.
The poetess of the Statue of Liberty.

Rogow, S. *Lillian Wald: The Nurse in Blue*. Philadelphia: Jewish Publication Society, 1966.
A beautifully written biography of the woman who founded the famous Henry Street Settlement House in New York and courageously battled poverty, suffering and disease all her life.

Vorspan, A. *Giants of Justice*. New York: Union of American Hebrew Congregations, 1960.
Profiles of 14 prominent Jews who have had an impact on American democracy.

Williams, B. *Lillian Wald, Angel of Henry Street.* New York: Messner, 1948.

The founder of the Henry Street Settlement House.

Wilson, J. H., Jr. *Albert A. Michelson.* New York: Messner, 1958.

America's first Nobel Prize physicist.

Wise, W. *Albert Einstein: Citizen of the World.* Philadelphia: Jewish Publication Society, 1960.

The author tells Einstein's life story with a simplicity and warmth that shines through every page.

Wise, W. *Silversmith of Old New York: Myer Myers.* Philadephia: Jewish Publication Society, 1959.

A Jewish artist and patriot in colonial New York.

Some Novels Dealing with Anti-Semitism in America

Bellow, S. *The Victim.* (N.A.L. and Compass paperbacks.)

Hobson, L. Z. *Gentleman's Agreement* (Avon paperback).

Katkov, N. *Eagle at My Eyes* and *A Little Sleep, A Little Slumber.* (Avon paperbacks).

Miller, A. *Focus.* (Avon paperback).

WHAT JEWS BELIEVE

Aims and Objectives

1. To examine the underlying beliefs of the Jewish religion concerning God and man, and their unique relationship to each other.
2. To illustrate the distinctiveness of Judaism—i.e., that it is a religion of historical evolution, and not one of creed or dogma.
3. To compare and contrast Jewish and Christian idea about monotheism, sin, the Messiah and other basic concepts.
4. To examine the Orthodox Jewish concept of Torah, or Law, and the role it plays as the foundation of religious behavior.
5. To come to grips with the fundamentally different ways in which Catholics and Jews approach the Jewish Bible.
6. To help the student perceive Jews as "the Jewish people"—i.e., as being different from other religious groups.
7. To examine the religious beliefs and the historical experiences of Jews that, taken together, have produced strong feelings of support for the State of Israel.
8. To evaluate the divisions in contemporary Judaism and to consider probable future trends.
9. To point out the emphasis placed by Judaism on actions (*mitzvot*) rather than on faith.
10. To consider the Jewish attitudes toward Jesus and toward Christianity.

Overview

Judaism is often described as "a way of life," or as "a religious civilization," in order to help explain its almost total lack of dogma, creed or catechism. It has been pointed out that, whereas the adherents of almost every world religion, or their ancestors, converted to that religion either at its founding or at some later time, Jews never "became" Jews; they just "were" Jews (i.e., they did not convert, but rather were all descendants of Abraham). Judaism evolved, and its truths and its teachings grew out of the experiences of the people known as Jews.

Nevertheless, as Rabbi Borowitz points out in the first part of his presentation on Jewish theology, certain central beliefs stand out boldly, and major thinkers have attempted to draw up articles of faith ever since the time that Judaism came into contact with speculative Greek thought.

One God

Although Judaism requires no declaration per se of faith in God, its underlying assumption is, clearly, belief in one God. This idea is economically expressed in the *Shema* (see "Jewish Worship").

On the simplest historical level, the declaration that God is One can be understood as a denial both of the pagan belief in many gods, and of the universe as something made up of multiple, hostile forces. But the *Shema* implies and teaches much more, as Rabbi Routtenberg and Rabbi Borowitz ("Aspects of Jewish Theology: Part I") point out. The teacher will want to examine Maimonides' Thirteen Articles of Faith ("Aspects: Part I"), which Rabbi Borowitz discusses, so as to understand some basic Jewish ideas about God. Instructive as well are the selections from Isaiah 45 (see "Aspects: Part I"), which convey in strikingly beautiful images the Jewish conception of the deity.

The important concepts for the teacher to stress can be briefly summarized as follows: God is one and indivisible; God has no bodily and no human characteristics; God cannot be represented in human form; God is the Creator of the universe and all that is in it; God is the Father of all mankind, and loves all His creatures.

It is important to emphasize the fact that the Jewish belief in one God includes the belief that God cares for man, and has entered into relationship with him. This leads us directly to the concept of the covenant.

The Covenant

The one God is transcendent, but He is not an impersonal force. His unity is not an abstraction—it is expressed in every aspect of Creation, and above all in man. The "mystery of God's love for man"—the astonishing fact that "God relates to man," and that He demands certain behavior from man—is stressed both in "Aspects: Part I" and in "What is Judaism?" by Rabbi Greenberg.

Rabbi Greenberg identifies the Exodus as the central experience in the relationship between God and the Jews. The theme of the Exodus is, in fact, a leitmotif of Judaism: the ideas it expresses are repeated over and over in the Bible, in later writings, in the prayers. God showed His love for the children of Israel by freeing them from the oppression, the injustice and the cruelty of life in ancient Egypt. Having released them from bondage, He brought them, through Moses, to Mount Sinai and there entered into a covenant with them. Through the covenant, God required of the children of Israel that they, and their descendants, exemplify in their daily lives the highest qualities of ethical perfection, and that they exercise the "freedom" He bestowed on them by choosing Good and by following His Torah.

The teacher will want to examine closely the two parts of "Aspects of Jewish Theology," in which Rabbi Borowitz traces the essential themes of the covenant. It might fairly be stated that the idea of the covenant is the single most important idea with regard to the Jewish religion and the Jewish people. Among the basic threads that make up the covenantal idea are these: mutuality—commitment of both God and man, extending to all generations; God's law—the Torah and other sacred writings; the peoplehood of Israel and the centrality of the Land of Israel; ultimate redemption—the Messiah and the messianic age. All of these themes will be explored in this guide.

Torah—God's Law

Torah is two things, essentially: it is the story of the children of Israel, the ancient forebears of today's Jews, and it is the "guidebook" that teaches the Jew how to live in God's way (see "Life Cycle of a Jew"). Unlike most guidebooks, however, the Torah is not always easy to understand. It has many layers of meaning, and many facets of truth. That is why it has required a vast literature—still being created today—to apply its teachings to life.

A popular textbook for Jewish students explains Torah this way:

"Perhaps the best way to think of Torah is a series of circles, one within the other. In the smallest circle, at the very heart of Torah, we have the Five Books of Moses, the first five books of the Bible.

"In the next circle we have the rest of the Bible: the Early and Later Prophets and that part of the Bible known as the Writings.

"In the third circle we have the Talmud, with its law, traditions and discussions.

"Still further out, we must include the many books written on Jewish Law and religious questions during the Middle Ages.

"Finally, there are modern books on the same topics, and some might even include books on other topics—even fiction or poetry—that were written in the spirit of Torah."*

Torah, then, is all the religious teachings of Judaism. According to Orthodox belief, when God gave Moses the Ten Commandments at Mount Sinai, He also gave him the entire Bible (Hebrew Scriptures) and all the later teachings, both legal and ethical. The implied meaning of this rather startling concept is that all the teachings, early and late, written (the Torah) and oral (the Talmud), are the word of God, and thus are equally binding on man (see "Judaism: Orthodox, Conservative, Reform").

Thus Torah is an evolving and ongoing relationship based upon the covenant and kept within the framework of the body of Jewish Law—*halachah.*

What the Law Means to Jews

Although Torah, in the broader sense, contains history, poetry, legend, parable, fable, maxims and philosophy, as well as laws, it is the Law that is the underpinning of the Covenant, the very basis of it. To a non-Jew, the Jewish emphasis on "law" (as opposed to "faith," for example) may be perplexing, for he is apt to conceive of "law" as something absolute, rigid, static, unfeeling—in short, the very antithesis of "love and concern."

Far from seeing obedience to the Law as harsh and repressive, however, Judaism has traditionally viewed such adherence as a glorious and joyous experience (see "Aspects of Jewish Theology"). The very word for the Law in Hebrew, *halachah,* means "walking," or "the way" —the way to live, the way to God (see "What is Judaism"). And, as Rabbi Borowitz points out, the holiday marking the end of the Torah-reading year is called "Simchat Torah"—or the "rejoicing of the Law."

Early Christian writers, like St. Paul, seemed to set up a dichotomy between Law and Faith, but such a contradiction does not exist in Judaism. In Judaism, law and faith are interwoven, they are one—and one without the other is a negation of "wholeness." God's law is love; it is His most precious gift to man, enabling him to climb the path to

---

*Singer, Howard, *With Mind and Heart,* United Synagogue Commission on Jewish Education, 1961, p. 137.

ethical perfection, to be more Godlike. Having the "right instincts" is not enough, says Judaism, for these are ultimately fallible. Man needs the objective guidelines of Divine Law to lead him.

How Jewish Law Developed

"What is Judaism?' traces the evolution of Jewish Law as the central factor in the Jewish religion. At the time of Jesus, the conflict that threatened the very existence of Judaism was between the Sadducee-priests who saw all of their religion in terms of a temple-based sacrificial cult based on a rigidly defined Scripture, and the Pharisee-rabbis who wanted Scripture to be applicable to all of life, wherever man lived.

As Rabbi Greenberg points out, it was the Pharisees who encouraged the notion of the Law as a changing, dynamic institution. If one accepted the Oral Law as being no less sacred than the biblical Written Law on which it was based, than the Law, in toto, would always meet the changing needs of man. "Torah was made for man, not man for Torah," they asserted.

As Rabbi Greenberg further demonstrates, it was this popular, in-terpretational view of the nature of Torah that enabled the Jewish religion not merely to survive the destruction of the Second Temple in 70 C.E. (Common Era) and the long Exile that followed, but to thrive as well. For this reason, Judaism owes a great debt to the Pharisees.

The legal principles and precedents hammered out by the rabbis proved capable of being applied to the ever-changing situations in which Jews, dispersed over the globe, were to find themselves. In every age, the laws were "relevant"—if not in their literal form, then through learned interpretation. But the underlying principles were always felt to come directly from the Torah, i.e., from God Himself.

As an example of "relevance," see "What is Judaism?" for the link-ing of the contemporary issue of "the right to strike" with a comparable talmudic discussion and with the "source" of the principle invoked, a verse in the Bible (Lev. 25:55).

The teacher will gain a clear sense of the evolutionary nature of Judaism from Rabbi Greenberg's analysis of the Responsa literature—the collected legal opinions of the rabbis from the tenth century on-ward—that deal with a vast and fascinating range of subjects. The point to be stressed here is that at no time in history could Judaism be con-sidered "ossified" or static. It was always in the process of adjusting to new situations and new demands. (For additional examples, see Biblio-graphy.)

Mitzvah

The purpose of rabbinic law was not to stultify life, but to enhance it. The rabbis believed that all of life is sacred, and that man should sanctify every aspect of his daily life through the performance of specific acts—*mitzvot* (plural of *mitzvah*). The *mitzvot* were intended to give concrete form to the lofty ideals of Scripture, especially those of the Prophets.

Rabbi Greenberg translates *mitzvah* as "a deed which fuses action and religious values in a single act." Rabbi Stuart Rosenberg defines it as "a proposition-in-action" or a "ritual of interpersonal behavior." *Mitzvah* is often rendered as "commandment" or "good deed," but these convey only partial meanings. This is what Rabbi Rosenberg has to say:

"The commandments of the Written Torah—the Pentateuch—had been very specific and detailed when it came to rules relating to the sacrificial laws and priestly regulations. But what precisely did it mean when it said: 'Honor thy father and thy mother'; or, 'Love thy neighbor as thyself'; or 'Remember that you were once slaves in the land of Egypt'? The rabbis deliberately concerned themselves with such questions, and the answers they gave made their Oral Torah into much more than a commentary or tradition. They deepened, humanized, and universalized it. As the priests had been concerned with codifying the rituals of the cult, the rabbis sought to codify love, loyalty and human compassion.

"In effect, they rebuilt the Jewish religion by translating what had been prophetic sentiment into a personal religion built on "propositions-in-action." Hospitality to wayfarers, visiting the sick, dowering the indigent bride, giving charity anonymously, attending the dead to the grave and helping to bring peace to those who lack it—these duties, for example, were never actually adumbrated in the Bible, although they are generally felt in spirit. The rabbis made them, and many like them, into new commandments, or *mitzvot,* and thus made communion with God an act that could and should be experienced everywhere and any time, with or without the Temple, the priests, or the sacrificial altar.*

It is important to emphasize that the spirit in which *mitzvot* are performed is as important as the acts themselves. Giving charity is a *mitzvah,* but *only* if one does it with a holy intention. To give charity grudgingly, or to embarrass the person who receives it, would be a desecration of God's name, and certainly not a sacred act.

---

*Rosenberg, Stuart E., *Judaism,* Paulist Press (paperback), pp. 44-45.

The teacher will want to take note of the fact that the discussion of Law as outlined in the preceding pages (and as explained by Rabbi Borowitz and by Rabbi Greenberg) represents the "classical" or traditional view. In modern times, Orthodox Judaism alone accepts the revealed nature of Torah, and teaches strict adherence to all the laws. Reform and Conservative Judaism have different views and teachings, while "secular" Jews have yet other approaches to the Bible. These varying beliefs are discussed in the section on "Orthodox, Conservative and Reform," and in the section on "The American Jews."

Sin and Atonement

The attitude of Judaism toward sin can be summed up, as Rabbi Borowitz indicates, in the verse from Genesis (4:7): ". . . . sin couches at the door, and unto you is its desire; *but you can rule over it."*

Man has within him the power to sin. This *yetzer ha-ra,* the "evil inclination," was created by God, together with *yetzer ha-tov,* the "good inclination," so that man should have freedom of choice, should be able to prove his ethical strength by "ruling over" sin.

In short, man is inherently neither righteous nor evil, but has the power to choose his course. The temptation to sin is ever present. No special "grace" is needed to redeem man from sin—rather, by his own efforts, the sinner must overcome temptation and atone for his wrongdoing. This view of man's nature was clearly enunciated by Maimonides, the great twelfth-century philosopher, in the *Mishneh Torah,* a legal commentary:

". . . Were God to decree that a man be righteous or wicked, or if there were anything in his basic constitution forcing him in either of the two ways . . . how could He have commanded us through the Prophets, act thus and not thus, mend your ways and do not go after your wickedness, if from his very creation his conduct had been decreed for him, or if his constitution would force him to do something he cannot resist? What place would there be for the whole of the Torah? Or by what justice and by what right could He punish the wicked or reward the righteous?" The concept of free will is thus basic, and stands in direct relationship with Divine Retribution.

Since, in the Jewish view, man stands in direct relationship with God, no intermediary is needed for man to atone and be forgiven. (See Isaiah 55:7.) Borrowing from the liturgy of Yom Kippur, man can atone for his sins through "repentance, prayer, and righteous living (good deeds)." Generally speaking, the rabbis distinguished between two categories of sin: sins against God (ritual transgressions) and sins against man (ethical transgressions). Sins against man must be forgiven by the person sinned against before seeking God's forgiveness; and the sinner must, where possible, make restitution.

The essence of atonement in Judaism is deed, not expression of faith. Confession, prayer and resolve to do better are important aspects of atonement—but not all. Man must change his ways, make good his wrongs, be different today from what he was yesterday, make himself "a new heart and a new spirit" (Ezek. 18:30).

(See the section in this Teachers' Guide on the Day of Atonement for additional explanation of this concept.)

Asceticism

In connection with a discussion of the concept of sin in Judaism, it should be noted that Judaism does not encourage or even approve of asceticism as a means of atonement or of righteous living. Judaism teaches that body and soul are one, that man worships God with his physical being as well as with his spiritual being. All of life is sacred, and every act can be a holy act.

The presentation in Rabbi Harlow's "Life Cycle of the Jew" stresses the role of marriage—which is considered not a "concession" to the weakness of the flesh (an idea that Jews reject), but an affirmation of the life force created by God. The rabbis taught that the very first commandment (*mitzvah*) in the Torah is: "Be fruitful and multiply" (Gen. 1:28).

Fasting is the only form of asceticism practiced formally, though throughout history there have been small groups and individuals (see Num. 6:1-21) that adopted other ascetic practices (for example, the Essenes). These groups were never in the mainstream of Judaism, however, and the ascetic viewpoint is basically inimical to the here-and-now and the joy-in-life outlook of Judaism.

Peoplehood

A non-Jew might well wonder at the inclusion of the concept "peoplehood" in a catalogue of basic Jewish beliefs, but as Rabbi Borowitz indicates ("Aspects of Jewish Theology: Part II"), the covenant with God *necessitates* the existence of the Jews *as a people,* for the covenant was made, not with individuals, but with the children of Israel collectively.

As is also made clear in the section on "The American Jew," Judaism cannot be adequately described as "a religion," nor can Jews be considered solely as believers in a particular religious system. The Jewish people has always seen itself *as a people*—no matter how numerous the countries in which they were dispersed, no matter how divergent their views on faith and practices. They are Jews by destiny, and in the case of most, by will.

Being a loyal member of the Jewish people does not mean, as some have claimed, being disloyal to one's country of residence. On the contrary, Jews have always been (when permitted) devoted, loyal and productive citizens in whatever country they were born or have lived.

At the same time—and there is no conflict involved—they are concerned about the welfare of their brothers everywhere, and they have a special interest in the State of Israel.

Non-Jews are frequently amazed at how passionately their Jewish friends feel about Israel or at how assiduously they raise funds for Jews in Israel and elsewhere. The explanation is quite simple: There are, all told, about 13 million Jews in the world, most of them concentrated in three communities: the United States—5½ million; Israel—2½ million; the Soviet Union—2½ million. (The remainder are scattered throughout the world.)

During World War II six million Jews, approximately *one-third* of the Jewish population *of the world,* were murdered. The Jewish people have never really fully recovered from that blow. That is why Jews react so strongly to threats against the 2½ million Jews in Israel. That is why the Jews of Israel have become such tenacious fighters. (See "Judaism: Orthodox, Conservative, Reform" and also the Teachers' Guide, "Writings of the Nazi Holocaust.")

It is something of an irony, perhaps, that the tragedies that have befallen Jews, the attempts made throughout history to destroy them, have in fact strengthened the bond of peoplehood and the conviction that Jews must survive. Certainly, the slaughter of six million Jews by the Nazis during World War II strengthened the bonds of fellowship between all Jews, no matter what their commitment to Jewish life. Faced with the awesomeness of that tragedy, Jews—and many non-Jews— rallied together to help the survivors. There was the unassailable fact that hundreds of thousands of Jews who had survived Hitler's ovens were homeless—nobody wanted them. That situation helped to bring about the establishment of the Jewish National Home, the modern State of Israel.

The Land of Israel

No other aspect of Judaism is so little understood as the relation of the *people* of Israel, the Jews, to the *land* of Israel—which today is a modern political state. Most Jews are strong supporters of that state, often passionate, in fact, and many non-Jews question this strong attachment. In the conflict between Israel and the Arabs, for example, while a majority of Americans are generally sympathetic to Israel, many question specific policies of Israel, some blame her for the Arab refugee problem, and still others believe our government should be more friendly to the Arabs.

The conflict between the Arabs and Israel is highly complex, and elaboration of it is not possible within the scope of this guide on the Jewish religion. What does concern us here is the way American Jews think about Israel and why. On the specific subject of the Arab-Israel conflict we can say that most Jews support Israel's struggle for survival, though there are occasional reservations about specific moves or policies. But, even when they are being critical, they talk as if it is a member of the family they are criticizing.

Here are some key attitudes that most American Jews have about Israel:

a) Israel must continue to exist—there is no thinkable alternative.
b) Israel wants peace—there is no advantage to her in warfare.
c) Israel and the Arab states could, if the Arabs wanted, live at peace—and the whole region would flourish.
d) Until the Arabs change their minds about destroying Israel, Israel must be prepared to defend herself.

To gain even a superficial grasp of these matters, both teacher and students will want to read one or more of the books on Israel listed under the heading, Israel, in the Bibliography at the end of this section. What we can try to do within the scope of this guide is to sketch some of the attitudes that Jews have about Israel, and trace the importance of the Land of Israel to Jewish religion and culture. We will also examine briefly the traditional Christian point of view toward the Land of Israel.

Historical and Religious Roots

From their earliest existence in the Land of Canaan, the Hebrews believed that the Lord had given the land to them "as an inheritance."

For well over a thousand years they lived in that land, much of the time as an autonomous kingdom. They were conquered and exiled by the Babylonians in 586 B.C.E., but many returned less than a century later and eventually established the Second Commonwealth. Then in 70 C.E. the legions of Rome overran Jerusalem, destroyed the Temples and scattered the people in exile. Though a community of Jews was always to be found in the Holy Land—at some periods they numbered in the hundreds, in others in the tens of thousands—the bulk of the Jewish people was soon dispersed over the globe. From 70 until the proclamation of the State of Israel in 1948—a span of 1,878 years—the thought, hope and prayer of "return to Zion" was a constant motif in Jewish worship, literature, folklore and song.

The very act of commemorating the destruction of Jerusalem assumed an almost obsessive force in Jewish life. The theme of Destruction went hand in hand with the theme of Return, and Jewish liturgy and ritual overflow with references to these events:

a) The Fast of Tisha B'Av.
b) The traditional words of comfort to a mourner: "May the Lord comfort you among all those that mourn for Zion and Jerusalem."
c) The breaking of a glass at the wedding ceremony (see "Life Cycle").
d) The wedding benediction, asking for "joy in Jerusalem" (*ibid.*).
e) The custom of placing a small bag of earth from the Holy Land in the coffin, for burial with the deceased.
f) In daily, Sabbath and Festival prayers: prayers for the redemption, recovery, prosperity and peace of Zion and Jerusalem.
g) Prayers for rain and dew, in accordance with the seasons in the Holy Land, not those of the land where the worshiper lives.
h) At the conclusion of the Seder when everyone says: *"L'Shana Haba'a B'Yerushalayim—Next Year in Jerusalem!"*

As Rabbi Borowitz makes clear ("Aspects: Part II"), the core of Jewish attachment to Israel is the covenant. Though the covenant is binding upon Jews no matter where they reside, it reaches its ultimate fulfillment in the land of Israel.

Thus, Israel has a meaning for Jews that is different from the meaning of the Holy Land to Christians and Moslems. For the latter groups, the land holds sacred shrines and memories, holy places that draw the faithful to visit at least once in a lifetime and to worship. For Jews, too, there are special holy places, and Jews everywhere hope to visit them at least once. In essence, however, all of the land (in Hebrew one can say, simply, *ha-aretz,* "the land," when speaking of Israel) is sacred, and to be there, especially to live there, is to fulfill a sacred duty.

Dr. Abraham J. Heschel's book *Israel: An Echo of Eternity* is especially recommended. It conveys, poetically and factually, the nature and history of Jewish attachment to Israel. The bond between the land and the people of Israel has many spiritual and mystical nuances which Dr. Heschel successfully captures.

How Christians Understand Israel

While some Christians have always encouraged Jewish aspirations to be restored to their homeland, seeing in this the fulfillment of God's promise, the large majority of non-Jews have viewed such an event with skepticism. Though expressing sympathy for the plight of Jews who were oppressed, they have not always understood the *necessity,* the *inevitability,* of Israel for the Jewish people, and that the two are inseparable, one from the other. Part of the difficulty has to do with the different ways in which Jews and Christians have, at times, read the Jewish Bible.

The Jew has always read his Bible as if it really happened, and he has been on intimate terms with its people, places and events. For some Christians the Hebrew Scriptures are the "old" Testament—merely a mosaic of foreshadows of Christ and the New Testament that followed. The Catholic Church has considered the Jewish Bible her own document and has, at times, theologically used it to bolster Christian teachings. However, while Christians view in faith the event of Christ and His Church as the high point of God's historical dealings with His people, study texts of the "Old Testament" used in modern Christian (including Catholic) high schools, colleges, seminaries, etc., do treat the Jewish Bible as the Jewish Bible—that is, as the inspired written expression of the faith-awareness on the part of Israel of God's historical, covenantal relationship with His chosen people. Such a popular text would be Bernhard Anderson's *Understanding the Old Testament* (Prentice-Hall, 1957). Anderson is Protestant.

To do justice to the Jewish Bible, educated Christians endeavor to grasp the literal sense of what the Jewish authors wrote. By literal sense we mean what the authors meant to say, or what God inspired them to say, in their own idiom. It would, of course, be ludicrous to suggest that Jews read the Bible only in a literal or fundamental sense; obviously they understand a great deal as being figurative, or as capable of interpretation on many different levels. Still, there is a "plain sense" in which

Jews basically accept the biblical word. (*Israel: An Echo of Eternity*—Allegorization and the Bible, pp. 139-144.)

This radical difference in understanding the words of the Jewish Bible—i.e., that Christians see an allegorical meaning beyond the literal sense of the Hebrew Scriptures—must be grappled with if there is to be a glimmer of understanding of this subject. For example, in a simply allegorical way, the Catholic reader of the Jewish Bible could discern that God gave the Israelites land and then took it away by causing exile or diaspora in history in order to prepare His people for Christ's announcement that God's kingdom is "not of this world"; but the Jewish person finds in his Scriptures literal promises that God's kingdom *is* of this world, and that it is somehow centered in the land of Israel.

Another obstacle to Christian understanding of the Jewish attitude to Israel is a theological one, namely, the belief that the Jews, as punishment for the Crucifixion, would not be restored to their ancient homeland. Dr. Heschel* concludes that this curse of wandering is not found in biblical or patristic sources—apart from individual Fathers of the Church. On the sore point of the responsibility of Jews for the death of Christ, Catholic teachers are called upon to realize that Christ died freely (John 10:17-18), and to make known the teaching of Vatican II: "Jews should not be presented as repudiated or cursed by God, as if such views followed from the Holy Scriptures. All should take pains, then, lest in catechetical instruction and in the preaching of God's Word they teach anything out of harmony with the truth of the gospel and the spirit of Christ" (*Declaration on the Relationship of the Church to Non-Christian Religions,* 4).

How the American Jew Sees Israel

Israel is an integral part of the system of beliefs of the observant or religious Jew. Among Jews who are not religiously Orthodox, however —and this probably means the majority—there are numerous shadings of opinion and support. At the opposite end of the scale from the Orthodox are assimilated Jews who have repudiated their Jewish identity (except perhaps in name only) and who may be indifferent to Israel or may even oppose her. In between are the vast numbers who are more or less religiously observant, more or less engaged in Jewish causes, and more or less committed to helping Israel and to identifying with the

---

Op. cit., pp. 161-67.

land and its culture. (See "Who is the American Jew?" and "What is Judaism?")

While the non-religious or "secular" Jew may deny the relevance or sacredness of the covenant as related to Israel, he may offer instead a different basis for his support. Any or all of these points might be used by him:

a) Jews feel responsible for each other; having all suffered, they are quick to extend a helping hand when fellow Jews are in trouble, whether it be in Israel, the Soviet Union or anywhere else.

b) Jews need a refuge; this is a purely pragmatic approach based on the fact of anti-Semitism in history. Even a superficial reading of Jewish history reveals that Jews have always been persecuted, whether they affirmed or denied their Jewishness. Jews have been killed, or degraded, or kicked from one country to another. Since the beginning of the twentieth century, it is only in the United States that a large Jewish community lived in peace. Yet the immigration quota system in force until recently in this country kept out thousands of Jews—and non-Jews— who were victims of Nazi persecution and had no place to go. The calamitous years of World War II convinced many Jews that Israel was a necessity.

c) Israel makes Jews "normal." A long-standing argument for the existence of a Jewish state has been that Jews need their own country in order to be like other peoples, to achieve a degree of normalcy, to cease being that enigmatic, feared, hated, shadowy figure of history—the Wandering Jew. Among the positive changes that are seen to take place when the Jews are restored to their land is the achieving of a "healthy" balance in occupational distribution. In Diaspora (or Exile), Jews have been almost entirely middle class, and limited largely to small businesses and the professions; in their own state, however, they are farmers, laborers and bus drivers as well as professors and storekeepers.

d) Israel gives the Jew a new, heroic image. The Jew perceives himself differently as a result of having his own state. The pallid talmudist of the ghetto has been transformed, as it were, into the brawny farmer and the superb fighting man. This latter figure arouses particular feelings of pride in Jews, who always tended to think of their people as possessing more brain than brawn. In Israel one sees strapping young natives of the land, blond and tanned, performing miraculous feats of building up the land, and prepared to die bravely to protect it. Jews may still wish to emphasize the intellectual and spiritual aspects of their culture, but they appreciate these newly acquired qualities. And they appreciate them precisely because, throughout the period of Exile, from 70 C.E. onward, these qualities were obliterated.

Zionism

The Jews have had a long history of living with oppression, exiled and reviled as they were in many lands. What sustained them, what kept them from disappearing altogether, was their faith that they were acting out their role in God's drama. They stuck doggedly to the script, following God's teachings and laws to the letter, believing firmly that Redemption would come when He so willed it. Even when faced with the most terrifying moment in Jewish history—the destruction by Hitler of six million Jews in World War II—the devout Jew went to his death reciting the *Shema,* the affirmation of God's existence.

For the non-religious Jew, and even for some believers, however, the submissiveness that had become a pattern of life was abhorrent. As far back as the early 1800's, there were those who believed that Jews had to take matters into their own hands, and seek to reestablish a Jewish homeland in Palestine. This was the impetus for Zionism, a political movement that arose in Europe in the middle of the nineteenth century, strongly influenced by the rise of nationalist movements everywhere.

The Zionists struggled for many years to bring about the establishment of the Jewish State. Many went as pioneers to the Holy Land, and by sheer sweat and muscle built flourishing settlements on land which they bought, piece by piece. Others worked to gain international support for the establishment of a Jewish homeland. Finally, in 1948, following the terrible holocaust of European Jewry, the independent State of Israel was established.

Messianism

Rabbi Borowitz discusses the varying conceptions of the Messiah and of the Messianic period ("Aspects of Jewish Theology," Part II), and cites a particularly interesting passage from Maimonides that lists some of the prerequisites for a Messiah, but is actually quite vague about what will occur when He comes. (Maimonides established the belief in the coming of the Messiah as one of his Thirteen Articles of Faith ["Aspects: Part I"] but this was one of the articles that was widely challenged by contemporary scholars.) In short, there has never been a unified and clearcut doctrine in Judaism about the coming of the Messiah or "the end of days"—but these concepts have persisted strongly, in one form or another.

Orthodox Jews today generally adhere to a belief in a personal Messiah, i.e., in a person "anointed" (the meaning of "messiah," *mashiach* in Hebrew) by God: He will come when Jews have become better Jews, and when the people of Israel are restored to their land. They also believe that the coming of the Messiah will bring about the resurrection of the dead.

However, most believing modern Jews today would probably tend to deny the belief in a personal Messiah, which they see rather as symbolizing a better age to come. They believe that the Kingdom of God will come to be—within history and on this earth, and that all men, laboring together, inspired by a belief in God, can bring it about.

Orthodox, Conservative, Reform

In this section we have been considering the basic beliefs of Judaism. Now we will briefly examine some of the divergent views that characterize Jews today, particularly in the United States.

The basic "platforms" of the three religious trends in American Judaism are presented in "Judaism: Orthodox, Conservative, Reform; though, as is indicated, changes have occurred since their writing, notably in the Reform movement's growing identification with the upbuilding of the State of Israel.

In size, the three groups are considered to be about equal; together, they represent somewhat more than half of this country's 5½ million Jews. How many of the "unaffiliated" would consider themselves "secular Jews," as defined by Dr. Wyschogrod, is not known. (An important source for most recent figures on, and analysis of, Jewish population and affiliation is the *American Jewish Year Book—see* Bibliography.)

In studying the three religious groupings, it should be stressed that though there are some very significant differences—notably over the question of the sanctity and authority of Torah—most of them occur in the area of practice and observance. In the area of belief, the three groups have more in common than their adherents themselves may realize. For example:

"All three groups assert that they believe in one God.

"All three believe that God is the Creator of the universe, that He is merciful and just, that He is a loving Father, and that He hears prayer.

"All three groups believe in the importance of Torah, although they interpret the Torah differently. Still, it's the same Torah that is taken out and read to the congregations of all three groups on the Sabbath and Holy Days.

"All three believe in the important task of the Jewish people, although, here again, each group may interpret that task differently.

"Even in the area of observances, it is important to remember that all three groups observe the same great holidays, although in different ways, and that even many of the prayers are the same."*

It is also suggested that the teacher read Chapter IV, "Modern Judaism," in *Judaism* (Deus Books) for a clear, concise, yet admirably detailed exposition of the development of the three major trends in present-day American Judaism.

Suggested Classroom Activities and Discussion Topics

These activities are suitable for use—with occasional modifications by Catholic, Protestant, and Jewish groups.

1. With the aim of establishing at least a rudimentary knowledge of the basic tenets of Judaism, assign either the entire class or else small groups to read and report on the various concepts included in this section. (A number of the suggested activities listed below may be used as individual assignments for a more thorough analysis of a specific concept.)

2. Invite a rabbi, a teacher in a Jewish parochial school or a rabbinical student to discuss his beliefs—how they relate to and differ from Catholicism, as well as other trends in Judaism. It is suggested that the class prepare questions, and if possible send them to the guest ahead of time. A follow-up question-and-answer period is strongly recommended.

3. Preparation of a glossary for class use. Have students compile terms as they proceed in their reading and research, and instruct them to include English as well as Hebrew terms (i.e., holocaust, diaspora, etc.) The final compilation might be mimeographed and

---

*Singer, Howard. *With Mind and Heart.* United Synagogue Commission on Jewish Education, 1961, p. 297.

distributed to the entire class. The glossary in this guide and in Stuart E. Rosenberg's *Judaism* should prove helpful in this activity.

4. Assign individuals or committees to report on the following topics: The Jewish Bible; The Pharisees; The Dead Sea Scrolls; Hassidism; Orthodox, Conservative and Reform Judaism; The Talmud; Religious Conversion.

5. *The Church and the Jews:* a symposium, or series of reports on this topic, focusing on such different periods of history as: The Medieval Period, Spanish Period, Modern Europe (including World War II) and America. (See the Teachers' Study Guide on "Jewish Stereotypes in English Literature: The Jew in the Middle Ages" from the series *The Image of the Jew in Literature;* and *The Jew in the Medieval World* by J. Marcus (Atheneum).

6. A report on *The Jews and the Crusades.* Historical sources (Jewish and Christian) as well as fictional accounts should be utilized in this connection. A committee might prepare a mock "You Are There" radio or TV presentation, centering around a specific episode. Similarly, a student could write up a particularly dramatic event of that period in the form of a newspaper report or editorial. (Consult Marcus, J. *The Jew in the Medieval World: A Source Book 315–1791.* Atheneum, 1969.)

7. Artistic projects such as murals, dioramas, collages and story illustrations should be strongly encouraged. Students might particularly enjoy trying to make montages representing Jewish symbols, ideas or historical events. The best samples of all this work may be posted on the bulletin board or on the walls of the classroom.

8. Have students select five passages (or "mottos") from the Jewish Bible that seem to them to reflect important values, and have them explain why. The more artistic students can be encouraged to make posters which incorporate a particularly apt verse.

9. Prepare a "living newspaper" on the subject of the Holy Land during the time of Jesus. (The books by Kotker and Rops listed at the end of this section will be particularly helpful in this regard.) Include political news, features, interviews, social and women's notes and, if possible, illustrations or cartoons. There are also possibilities here for some form of dramatic presentation.

10. *Jewish Music.* Play selected recordings of various types of Jewish music: *Yiddish folk songs* (songs of Jews originating in Russia,

Poland and other European countries); *Sephardic folk songs* (songs of Jews originating in North Africa, the Middle East and certain Southern European countries. Jews from these areas did not speak Yiddish, but Ladino—their own dialect, which is based on Spanish); *modern Israeli songs*—in Hebrew; *songs and dances of the Hassidim; music of the synagogue.* (See list of suggested recordings in "Additional Resources.")

11. *Films and Film Strips.* See "Additional Resources."

12. *One God.* Have students look up in the Jewish Bible the text of the full *Shema*—the basic catechism or "watchword" of the Jewish faith: Deut. 6:4-9; Deut. 11:13-21; and Num. 15:37-41. The teacher may wish to have the passages mimeographed for the entire class.

13. The first sentence of the *Shema* (pronounced with the accent on the second syllable) is well known: "Hear, O Israel, the Lord is our God, the Lord is One." Religiously observant Jews recite these words at daily prayers, before going to sleep at night and on their deathbeds. In addition, Jewish martyrs throughout history proclaimed the *Shema* as they went to their deaths.

When the student reads the entire declaration, he may be surprised to find that the words are so simple and do not, on the face of it, seem to say very much. Why then are these few words so important to Jews that many have chosen to die for them? What are some of the deeper meanings of the *Shema* and what important ideas about Judaism can be deduced from it? Is there a difference between the "One God" whom Christians believe in and the "One God" Jews worship?

14. *Jewish law.* When this subject is mentioned, many people think of the biblical phrase, "an eye for an eye, a tooth for a tooth." Ask students what their *first* reaction is when they hear this phrase?

Then have them look up the laws in Exodus 21:12-27 (These include the well known "eye for an eye.") Does this passage add anything to their understanding of the concept?

Finally, have them find out all they can about how these laws were interpreted and practiced at various periods in Jewish history. Compare them with the laws of other ancient peoples—the Greeks, Romans, Babylonians, etc.

15. Make a study of two famous Jewish stereotypes in literature, Shylock in *The Merchant of Venice* and Fagin in *Oliver Twist.* How

does the character of Shylock in Shakespeare's *Merchant of Venice* reflect a misunderstanding of the biblical law cited in Exodus 21:24-5? Indicate what qualities were considered "typical" of Jews and were used by Shakespeare and then by Dickens (who lived over 200 years apart!). Have students report on these stereotyped figures against the background of *their historical settings*.

(The teacher is referred to the Teachers' Study Guide on "Jewish Stereotypes in English Literature: Shylock and Fagin" from the series, The Image of the Jew in Literature, published by the Catholic Archdiocese of New York and the Anti-Defamation League of B'nai B'rith.)

16. *"Mitzvah"—the religious deed.* The following activity may aid students in understanding the concept of *mitzvah,* which is considered by many scholars to be the basis of Judaism. In addition to reading relevant source material, have students look up all ten biblical references listed below. When students have determined exactly what religious duty (or duties) is called forth in each passage, let them divide the *mitzvot* into two categories: duties to God (which may also be called ritual duties, and include observance of holidays and prayers), and duties to man (or "ethical duties").
Here are the biblical references:

> Exodus 12, verses 18, 19
> Exodus 20, verses 4, 5, 8, 12
> Exodus 23, verse 5
> Leviticus 16, verse 29
> Leviticus 19, verses 9, 13, 15, 16, 34, 36
> Leviticus 22, verse 32
> Numbers 15, verse 38
> Deuteronomy 6, verses 5, 7, 9
> Deuteronomy 8, verse 10
> Deuteronomy 23, verse 24

Then have students discuss whether Jews today observe the various ritual commandments, and if so, how. If necessary, assign individual students to carry out research on this subject. At the same time, explain that the "ethical" commandments of the Jewish Bible are considered by Jews to be as binding today as when they were written—even though life situations are very different. Stimulate students to create contemporary situations to which the ancient biblical verses might apply. For example, passage 3 in the above list—Exod. 23:5—speaks of "the ass of him that hateth thee lying under its burden"—which might be understood today as "the loaded truck of a rival storekeeper which has a flat tire," etc.

17. Judaism does not require a man "to be good" in a general way, but rather to fulfill specific *mitzvot,* or ethical acts—even when he doesn't really want to! Among these *mitzvot* are: comforting the mourner, visiting the sick, rejoicing with bride and groom, respecting one's parents. What is more, Jewish law is quite specific about the performance of each *mitzvah*—for example, how long one may visit a sick person so as not to tire him.

Have students consider the merits and faults in this system of eliciting ethical behavior from an individual. Is there any value in performing a good deed, not because you sincerely want to but because you are commanded to? How do we learn ethical behavior in the first place? What is meant by the statement that the precept of the *mitzvah* is the good act rather than the correct concept? Do you agree?

18. *Sin.* The following story from the Talmud, which should be read to the class, is intended to demonstrate how God rewards the righteous and punishes the sinful:

> On Judgment Day the Lord decided to slay Temptation ("the evil inclination") before the eyes of a sinner and of a righteous man. Both men wept at what they saw—but each one saw something different! To the righteous man, Temptation appeared as an enormous mountain. "Oh Lord," he cried out, "how did I have the strength, every day of my life, to overcome that mighty mountain?" To the wicked man, however, Temptation appeared as nothing more than a single hair of a man's head. "Oh Lord," he wept, "why was I not even able to conquer that tiny hair?"

After the reading, ask the class the following questions: What do you think of the "reward" and "punishment" meted out by God in this tale? Can you draw any conclusions from this story about the Jewish view of man's nature and his behavior?

Note that nothing is said in the above story about the role that God might have played in either the sinner's or the good man's life. Is there any Catholic notion that man can overcome temptation completely on his own? What is the Jewish view? What are Protestant views?

19. *Covenant.* Have a number of students read Exodus 19:5-6 and write down or report orally their *first* thoughts about the passage. Then let them answer the question—Do Jews still believe that they have this covenantal relationship with God?

20. *Report on the Orthodox, Conservative, Reform and "Secular" trends in Judaism today.* A class report may include discussion of the following questions:

    a. For what reasons did the Conservative and Reform movements come into being?
    b. How would each of the three trends describe "a good Jew"? (List specific characteristics and practices.)
    c. How would a "secular" Jew describe his beliefs and attitudes?
    d. Can you list Jews you know under the headings "Orthodox," "Conservative," "Reform" or "Secular"? If you can, explain why you have assigned individuals to one category or another.
    e. Regardless of affiliation or "label," what factors, in your judgment, bind all Jews together?

21. *Messiah.* Present the following statement to the class as a topic for research and discussion: "As far as Jews are concerned, the Messiah has not yet come."

    Follow this up with such questions as: Is the above a true statement of Jewish belief? What exactly do Jews believe about the Messiah? Can you explain why most Jews living at the time of Jesus did not consider him to be the Messiah? Why were many of them prepared to believe in "false" Messiahs such as Sabbatai Zevi in Turkey during the seventeenth century?

22. *The Nazi Holocaust and its effects on the Jewish psyche.* This important subject may be approached most interestingly through a study of Jewish legends, which also provide insight into the Jewish (especially Hassidic) view of God and his role in history. The teacher is referred to the filmed programs and accompanying Teachers' Study Guides on "Jewish Legends" by Eli Wiesel, and "Writings of the Nazi Holocaust" by Ernst Pawel, in the series The Image of the Jew in Literature, published by the Archdiocese of New York and the Anti-Defamation League of B'nai B'rith.

    This subject can also be related to the section under Israel and some of the activities on Israel listed below. What connections, if any, exist between the Holocaust and the rise of Israel to national statehood? What effect do you think the Holocaust has had on

Jews all over the world? (*See* also Dore Schary's lecture "Who is the American Jew?")

Finally, Emil Fackenheim, the Jewish theologian, has spoken of a 614th commandment (a reference to the tradition that there are 613 commandments found in the Torah). It is "not to hand Hitler another victory." And it is surely no accident that the most widely supported charity in the American Jewish community is the United Jewish Appeal, which earmarks 80% of its funds for the rehabilitation of Jews in Israel. Comment and discuss.

23. *Land of Israel.* Have students look up the following biblical passages: Gen. 28:10-22. Jer. 31:15-17. Isaiah 2:2-4, 52:9-10, 62:1-9. Ezek. 37:1-14. Psalm 137:1-6 , 122.

Have students explain the literal meaning first, and then the allegorical or "fuller" meaning. Let them do this on their own, making sure they understand that Jews accept the "plain sense" of these verses. Afterward, student should consult standard commentaries and report back their findings. (Soncino Books of the Bible contain standard Jewish commentaries. Modern Catholic sources would be the introduction and footnotes of *The Jerusalem Bible* [Doubleday, 1966] and *The Jerome Biblical Commentary* [Prentice-Hall, 1968]. The Anchor Bible [Doubleday] contains translations and commentaries by Protestant, Catholic and Jewish scholars.)

24. Write this quotation on the board or have it duplicated and distributed to students:

> "Even those who believe that God is everywhere set aside a place for a sanctuary. For the sacred to be sensed at all moments everywhere, it must also at this moment be somewhere." (A. J. Heschel, *Israel: An Echo of Eternity,* Noonday Press, 1969, page 11.)

Ask students to discuss, in writing or orally, the question: How does the above statement apply to the Jewish need to inhabit Israel?

25. During the June 1967 war in the Middle East, the Jews recaptured the Old City of Jerusalem which they had lost in 1948. It was reported at the time that the general who led the Israelis, a non-religious Jew, stood before the Western Wall of the ancient Temple and wept; yet said he did not know why he was weeping.

Ask for student opinion about this incident. Do students know non-religious Jews who strongly support Israel? Why do they feel the way they do? Why did the recapture of Jerusalem represent more than just another military victory to the Israeli general?

26. Many Irish Catholics in this country ardently support the cause of Catholic civil rights in Northern Ireland. Can you compare such support to that given by Jews to the State of Israel? Is any disloyalty to the United States implied when an American rallies strongly to a cause he believes just, though it be in another country?

27. If a Jew became President of the United States, would there be any question in people's minds about his loyalty? Was there any basis for the fears, publicly expressed, that John F. Kennedy would decide in conscience first as a Catholic, and then as an American—that is, that he would have prior allegiance to the Pope and the Vatican?

28. Considering that Jews have had a long history of wandering and of being persecuted, it is astonishing not only that they have survived, but that, in a general way, they seem to have positive attitudes about life. Discuss the possible reasons for the survival of the Jewish people, and ask students to relate this question to the Jewish conception of the Messiah and the Messianic Age.

29. Jewish belief is oriented toward the here-and-now, and emphasizes present life as all important. Compare and contrast this with those strands in Catholic belief that are more ascetically and future-world oriented.

30. The migration of Jews from all over the world to Israel has often been referred to as "the ingathering of the exiles." What does this mean? Where does the expression come from?

Bibliography

The following is a selected listing of books and other source material, mostly from Jewish sources, that are recommended for a study of the Jewish religion. For a more comprehensive bibliography, the teacher may wish to send for *A Bibliography on Judaism and Jewish-Christian Relations,* published by the Anti-Defamation League, 315 Lexington Avenue, New York, N.Y. 10016 (price: $1.00).

1—Indicates books suggested for the average high school student
2—Indicates books suggested for the superior high school student
3—indicates books suggested for the average teacher
4—Indicates books suggested for further reading

Jewish Religion and Philosophy

4 Baeck, L. *The Essence of Judaism.* New York: Schocken, 1961 (paperback).
> A difficult but important study by a leading liberal thinker of the underlying ideas of Judaism and their development.

3 Belkin, S. *In His Image.* New York: Abelard-Schuman, 1961.
> The president of Yeshiva University, an Orthodox scholar, presents his approach to rabbinic concepts and theology.

2 Hertzberg, A. editor. *Judaism* (Great Religions of Modern Man Series). New York: Braziller, 1962. (Also in paperback.)
> A conceptual anthology of Jewish literature dealing with the basic values of Judaism. Includes sections on the Jewish People, God, Torah, Land, Doctrine. Highly recommended.

3 Heschel, A. J. (F. A. Rothschild, editor). *Between God and Man: An Interpretation of Judaism* (paperback). New York: Free Press
> A selection of Prof. Heschel's writings presenting the substance of his understanding of Judaism, plus an intellectual biographical essay by the editor.

4 Heschel, A. J. *God in Search of Man.* Philadelphia: Jewish Publication Society, 1963. (Also in paperback.)
> A major theological, philosophical statement by the eminent Jewish theologian.

1 Kertzer, M. *What Is a Jew?* New York: Collier Books (paperback).
> An attempt to delineate some of the basic characteristics of the Jewish religion and the Jewish people.

1 Plaut, G. *Your Neighbor Is a Jew.* Philadelphia: Pilgrim Press, 1968 (paperback).

A collection of short, lively articles by a leading Reform rabbi, dealing with aspects of Jewish belief, holidays, and customs, as well as contemporary issues of a general nature. Good reading for all.

2   Rosenberg, S. *Judaism*. Glen Rock, N.J.: Deus Books, 1966 (paperback). This concise, readable treatment of Judaism, written by a rabbi especially for Catholic readers, could well serve as a text for high-school students. Includes the development of Judaism from biblical times to the present; Jewish worship and the holidays; rituals of Jewish life; and Jewish views on various theologoical concepts.

4   Schechter, S. *Studies in Judaism*. New York: Atheneum, 1970. Scholarly and superbly readable accounts of Jewish history and thought, including essays on Hasidism, the Bible, the Talmud and the history of Jewish tradition. Originally printed 1896-1919.

2   Singer, H. *With Mind and Heart*. New York: United Synagogue Commission on Jewish Education, 1961. A fine textbook for Jewish teenagers about their religion that may also be of interest to non-Jewish youth.

Judaism and Christianity

3   Abbott, W. M., S. J., editor. *The Documents of Vatican II*. New York: Herder and Herder, Associated Press, 1966. For each document there are an introduction, illuminative footnotes and a response by a non-Catholic. See especially the *Declaration on the Relation of the Church to Non-Christian Religions* as it relates to Jews, pp. 663-667.

4   Baeck, L. *Judaism and Christianity*. Philadelphia: Jewish Publication Society, 1958. (Also in paperback.) Five scholarly essays on the different attitudes and institutions of two religions by a leading theologian. Difficult but important.

4   Buber, M. *Two Types of Faith: The Interpenetration of Judaism and Christianity*. New York: Harper & Row, 1961. (Also in paperback.) A theological inquiry into Pharisaic Judaism and early Christianity presenting the differences and similarities of the two types of faith.

4   Cooke, B., S. J. "Christ in Scripture," in *Studies in Salvation History*. Salm, L., F.S.C., edition Englewood Cliffs, Prentice-Hall, 1964. This article, in part, asks Catholics to be disabused on the point of seeing isolated texts of the Jewish Bible as pointing clearly to Christ.

3   Daniel-Rops, H. *Daily Life in the Time of Jesus*. Mentor-Omega Book, 1964.

4   Katz, J. *Exclusiveness and Tolerance: Studies in Jewish-Gentile Relations in Medieval and Modern Times*. Oxford University Press, 1961. (Also available in paperback.) Jewish attitudes to the non-Jewish environment from the Middle Ages to the 18th century. A scholarly and important study .

1 Kotker, N. *The Holy Land in the Time of Jesus.* New York: Harper &
   Row, 1967.
   A vivid account, eminently readable and beautifully illustrated, of
   the Holy Land in Jesus' time as well as of the momentous events
   of the first century.

4 Sandmel, S. *We Jews and Jesus.* Oxford University Press, 1965.
   A non-technical, informed book on the Jewish attitude toward
   Jesus—throughout history and in the light of modern scholarship.

3 Silver, A. H. *Where Judaism Differed.* Philadelphia: Jewish Publication
   Society, 1957.
   A well written statement of the great insights and ethical teachings
   of Judaism by a leading Jewish spokesman of the twentieth-century.

Israel

1 Edelman, L. *Israel—New People in an Old Land.* New York: Thomas
   Nelson, 1969 (revised edition).
   Intended to be a basic book for the public schools, it treats fully
   and sensitively the events of June, 1967.

1 Essrig, H. and A. Segal, *Israel Today.* New York: Union of American
   Hebrew Congregations, 1968.
   The emphasis is on the contemporary situation in Israel. A comprehensive Teacher's Book, with a 1969 supplement, should prove
   helpful.

2 Hertzberg, A. ed. *The Zionist Idea: A Historical Analysis and Reader.*
   New York: Atheneum, 1969. (Also in paperback.)
   Highly recommended. An anthology of writings by Zionist thinkers
   and leaders, with an introductory essay by the editor .

3 Heschel, A. J. *Israel: An Echo of Eternity.* New York: Farrar, Straus
   and Giroux, 1969. (Also in paperback.)
   Highly recommended, a historical and theological account of the
   meaning of the Land of Israel to Jews and Judaism.

1 Levin, M. *The Story of Israel.* New York: G. P. Putnam's Sons, 1966.
   (Also in paperback.)
   A vivid account, written especially for young people, of the history
   of the modern State of Israel, tracing its development from Biblical
   times to the present.

Bibles

3 Cohen, A., ed. *Soncino Books of the Bible;* 14 volumes. New York:
   Soncino Press, 1950. (Most Jewish Congregational libraries have a set.)
   A highly recommended edition of the complete Jewish Bible; the
   Hebrew text, an English translation, and a commentary based on
   the traditional commentators.

1 *The Holy Scriptures According to the Masoretic Text.* Philadelphia:
   Jewish Publication Society, 1917.

This is the authoritative Bible used by most English-speaking Jews.

4   Anderson, B. *Understanding the Old Testament*. New York: Prentice-Hall. 1957.

The author, a Protestant, traces the literary and theological development of the Jewish Bible within the framework of Israel's development as a community. Significantly, this excellent work begins with the Exodus experience.

4   Brown, R. E., S. S., Fitzmyer, J. A., S. J., Murphy, R. E., O. Carm. *et al.* eds. *The Jerome Bible Commentary.* New York: Prentice-Hall, 1968.

A superior, chapter-and-verse commentary on the whole Bible produced by Catholic scholars; it contains a wealth of contemporary interpretation.

4   Ellis, P. C. SS. R. *The Men and Message of the Old Testament*. Collegeville, Minn.: The Liturgical Press, 1963.

A book-by-book explanation of the Jewish Bible by a Catholic scholar. At the end of each section, the author exegetes given Psalms as they apply to certain periods of Israel's development.

4   Hartmann, L. C. SS. R., editor. *Encyclopedic Dictionary of the Bible*. New York: McGraw-Hill, 1963.

An excellent, scholarly compendium of knowledge of the Jewish Bible and the New Testament by Catholic scholars. (*See* also McKenzie below.)

3   Jones, A. *et al.*, editors. *The Jerusalem Bible*. New York: Doubleday, 1966.

An excellent Catholic Bible in every way: text, introductions and footnotes.

3   McKenzie, J. L. S. J. *Dictionary of the Bible*. New York: Bruce, 1965.

Like Hartman's work above, an excellent compendium, but less technical and more readable.

4   McKenzie, J. L. S. J. *The Two-Edged Sword*. New York: Bruce, 1956. (Also in paperback.)

In topical fashion the author sets forth the religious ideas and values of the Jewish Bible with modern thought.

3   Tos, A. J. *Approaches to the Bible: The Old Testament*. New York: Prentice-Hall, 1963.

An introduction to Christian approaches to the Jewish Bible in the perspective of Salvation-History. The author respects the literal meanings of the Hebrew scriptures, but adds the "fuller" senses implied in Christian belief.

JEWISH WORSHIP AND THE JEWISH YEAR

Aims and Objectives

1. To afford the Christian student with basic knowledge about the Jewish holidays and their observance.
2. To illustrate the general structure of synagogue worship and its history.
3. To compare specific elements of Catholic or Protestant and Jewish worship.
4. To let the student experience, at first hand, Jewish worship or Jewish home observance of the Sabbath and holidays.
5. To point out the differences between Orthodox, Conservative and Reform worship forms.
6. To consider the ethical teachings, both implicit and explicit, in the festivals of Passover, Hanukkah and other holy days.
7. To indicate the emphasis given to the Land of Israel and the people of Israel in Jewish worship and in holiday observances.

Overview

The Synagogue

To a Christian who has had limited opportunity to observe Jewish life, the synagogue and its worship may seem totally foreign. The outward appearance of the synagogue building and of the sanctuary, the language of the prayers and the sound of the chants, the skullcaps and prayer shawls worn by the men, and in many cases the overall air of relative informality—all are in sharp contrast to the church and to the Mass. And yet, did not the Mass grow out of synagogue worship and the observance of the *Seder?*

The fact is that, despite their many differences, both superficial and substantive, a closer view of the synagogue and the church will reveal their common base.

Its Development

The Jews did not always worship in synagogues. During their wanderings through the desert and in their early days in the Holy Land, they performed their religious obligations before the "Ark of the Law," which was built to house the holy tablets of the Ten Commandments. The Ark was kept in a tent or in a temporary tabernacle. Later, King Solomon built a magnificent temple on Mount Zion in Jerusalem, with a special room set aside for the Ark. The Jews worshipped in Solomon's temple for about 350 years, until 586 B.C.E. In that year Nebuchadnezzar, the king of Babylonia, looted the Temple and destroyed it. As a consequence, the Jews lost not only their place of worship, but their homeland.

Deprived of their Temple and of almost all their ritual equipment, the Jews created new ways to observe their ancient faith. They began to meet in one another's homes; to sing the songs of the Temple on Sabbaths and Holy Days; to read and discuss the holy scrolls they had salvaged from Jerusalem and to pray for the time when they could return. When the gatherings became too large for private homes, they built special halls for the meetings. Such a gathering place was called *Beth Knesset* (house of assembly), and the Greeks translated this into synagogue.

When the Jews were permitted to return to Jerusalem after some 50 years of exile, they immediately started to build a new Temple on Mt. Zion; however, the tradition started in Babylonia was continued. Although the Temple was still regarded as the House of the Lord, the Jews established a great many synagogues throughout the Holy Land. In fact, it was in the synagogue that Jesus preached to his fellow Jews.

By the time of Jesus and Paul, the synagogue served many functions. It was the house of study of the Law and the Prophets; it was a community center for public meetings; it was used for the distribution of charity to the poor, and for the shelter and care of strangers. In short, the synagogue became a fixed and secure tradition.

Today, non-Jews are sometimes confused about the names by which Jews call their houses of worship—and there is some basis for such confusion. Reform Judaism introduced the designation "temple" for its synagogues, and at one time this was a clear mark of identification. (To a certain extent it still is, but not reliably so.) Some Conservative congregations now refer to themselves as "temple" and some Reform "temples" have become "synagogues." Sometimes, too, a synagogue is called "The Jewish Center," which is often a sign that the congregation is Conservative. No matter what the name, though, all Jewish houses of worship are synagogues, and there is nowhere a "temple" such as existed in the days of Solomon or Herod.

Inside the Synagogue

Attached to the right hand doorpost of the synagogue entrance is a most familiar Jewish symbol—the *mezzuzah*. (see "Jewish Worship.")

The sanctuary, where synagogue worship is conducted, generally faces east, in the direction of Jerusalem.* At the front of the sanctuary is a raised platform, in the very center of which is the Ark, covered by an embroidered curtain. The Ark and the curtain derive from the Tabernacle as described in the Bible (Exodus 26:31-34). Inside the Ark repose Torah scrolls, each containing the Five Books of Moses, while above it there are often two tablets with Hebrew letters on them— abbreviations of the Ten Commandments. A constantly burning lamp hangs in front of the Ark—the Eternal Light (*Ner Tamid*).

On the platform or dais there is a reading table or desk on which the Torah is placed. And in many synagogues there are two Menorot (seven-branched candelabra), reminiscent of the candelabra used in the ancient Temple in Jerusalem.

The Synagogue Service and the Prayerbook

"Jewish Worship" by Rabbi Routtenberg describes the daily, Sabbath and Festival services, and analyzes the essential elements in the liturgy: (1) the *Shema,* the declaration of belief in God's unity; (2) the *Amidah,* the Standing Prayer, and (3) the reading of the Torah.

A number of elements in Catholic prayer stem directly from Jewish prayer. The most obvious point of commonality is, of course, the Psalms, which are central both to the *Siddur* (the Jewish Prayer Book), and to forms of Catholic worship. Psalms are plentiful among the song and response parts of the Catholic Missal. In fact, the Psalms, prayers, scriptural readings and homily that constitute the Liturgy of the Word, or forepart of the Mass, were maintained by early Jewish converts to Christianity who frequented the synagogues, apart from celebrating the Liturgy of the Eucharist in private homes. The format of this forepart of the Mass has changed very little in Catholic worship down through the centuries. Even the Liturgy of the Eucharist begins with a doxology, the Thrice Holy, taken from Isaiah. Psalms form the body of the Divine Office. The Magnificat of Vespers is based on the Jewish Bible. Jesus

---

*There are often many other rooms in the synagogue building: classrooms for children and adults, and meeting rooms for various leisure-time activities. Now, as before, the synagogue is a gathering place for the Jews of the neighborhood or community.

taught the "Our Father" in the language of Hebrew Scriptures. Psalms are also prominent in the Protestant Book of Common Prayer. Historically, the 150 Aves of the complete rosary arose from a monastic substitution for the full 150 songs of the Hebrew Psalter.

Other notable examples of commonality are that elements of the *Shema*—"Hear, O Israel, the Lord our God, the Lord is One" (Deut. 6:4 and Lev. 19:18) are to be found, in one form or another, in Christian prayer, and that the very chant which is used in the reading of the Torah and which was passed down from ancient times, is the forerunner of Gregorian chant—one of the earliest forms of Church music.

Orthodox, Conservative and Reform

The ideologies of the three major "trends" in Judaism are discussed in the lecture "Judaism: Orthodox, Conservative, Reform" and in Part II of this Teachers' Guide, but in this section on worship it is appropriate to point to some of the specific distinguishing features of each.

In Orthodox and Conservative congregations the men wear *yarmulkes* (skullcaps) during prayer, following the manner in which people in the Near East still show respect and reverence. In addition, the Orthodox and Conservative Jew wears a prayer shawl with fringes, called a *tallit*. In most Reform congregations, only the rabbis still wear the traditional vestments.

Organs or other instrumental music are part of most Reform and Conservative services. Orthodox synagogues, however, regard the playing of instuments as a violation of Sabbath and Festival law. Another reason for prohibiting instrumental music is to demonstrate that the members of the congregation are in mourning for the destroyed Temple in Jerusalem. Orthodox synagogues still maintain separate sections of the sanctuary for men and women (as was the practice during the days of the Temple). In Conservative and Reform worship, however, they are together.

In terms of the actual worship, it is important to point out that its very style tends to vary considerably from synagogue to synagogue, just as it might, say, from an important metropolitan cathedral to a village church. A small, Orthodox synagogue (*shul,* in Yiddish) tends to be extremely informal, may seem, perhaps, even chaotic. The individual worshiper knows the prayers intimately and chants them aloud at his own pace, almost oblivious to those around him. In contrast, a Reform or Conservative congregation, or a large Orthodox one, is almost certain to worship in an atmosphere of decorum, in which the cantor and rabbi lead the worship, while individuals pray either in unison or in silent devotion.

Another distinction is that the Orthodox service uses Hebrew almost exclusively, whereas the Reform service is conducted mostly in English. As for the Conservative service, it is likely to use both languages in roughly equal proportions.

The role of Hebrew in Jewish worship and in Jewish culture generally is of paramount importance. Unlike Latin, Hebrew has always been a "living" language, and one, incidentally, which experienced a phenomenal renascence through the rebirth of Israel. Throughout the nearly two thousand years of Exile, Hebrew was kept alive as a language not only of prayer, but of philosophy, law and literature as well. There are scholars who maintain that those communities that abandoned Hebrew teaching and usage, were quick to assimilate and lose their Jewishness. In any case, for the Jew, Hebrew is definitely a living link with his past, all the way back to the Bible.

The Rabbi

Although the rabbi usually officiates during services by leading the prayers and delivering the sermon, the people as a whole commune directly with God. (All Jews, including the rabbi, are responsible to God for their individual acts.)

The rabbi is the Jewish religious leader, and devotes his entire energies to the spiritual needs of his community. In ancient times, however, the rabbinate was not a full-time vocation. Then the people simply appointed the most respected scholar in the community to guide them. The latter made his living like other people, either by working in the fields, or at a trade or profession. He was called *rav* or rabbi (which means teacher) as a mark of respect for his learning, knowledge and piety.

As the synagogue became the center of life in the Jewish community, seminaries were established to train people for the rabbinate. Today the title "Rabbi" is reserved for properly ordained graduates of such schools. In most seminaries rabbinical students are admitted into training after they have acquired their college degrees. They then undergo a rigorous four- to six-year period of Judaic study and spiritual preparation. Rabbis are encouraged to marry and raise families.

For an analysis in depth of the origins and significance of the synagogue and the rabbinate, two primary institutions in Jewish life, we recommend especially *Judaism* by Stuart Rosenberg. Other sources are listed in the Bibliography.

The Sabbath

The Sabbath has always been considered the most important of all Jewish holy days. The Sabbath alone is mentioned in the Ten Commandments, wherein the Jewish people were enjoined to "remember the Sabbath day to keep it holy." The Sabbath is considered to be a "foretaste" of the bliss the righteous will find in the world to come. For, on the Sabbath, the world is at peace and at one in its devotion to God.

On the Sabbath, Jews recall the creation of the world. Just as the Almighty created the world in six days and rested on the seventh, so man is to rest on this day to emulate His pattern. By working six days of the week, man glorifies the dignity of labor; and, by resting on the Sabbath, he reaffirms the sanctity of God and the dignity of man. But, since the mere cessation of labor only serves the needs of the body, proper observance of the Sabbath demands more. Thus, prayer, study and contemplation, as well as sweetness and joy in family associations are the traditional, recommended practices for the Sabbath day. (See "Life Cycle of the Jew".)

Jews observe the Sabbath in different ways. Orthodox Jews will not ride on the Sabbath, nor will they kindle a light. Work, the exchange of money, financial activity of any kind is forbidden. Conservative and Reform Jews, who interpret the biblical injunctions more liberally, do not restrict their actions to the same degree. Some Jews go to synagogue services on Friday evenings before supper, some after supper, others attend services on Saturday morning. (Some Jews, of course, do not observe the Sabbath at all.)

The Jewish Calendar

Unlike the civil calendar, the Jewish calendar takes into consideration the lunar as well as the solar cycle. Thus, Jewish holidays begin in the evening, when the sun sets, instead of at daybreak, when the sun rises, or at midnight. Jewish holidays do not always fall on the same civil calendar date each year, for the lunar cycle does not have as many days each month as does the solar cycle. The Jewish calendar, therefore, falls behind the civil calendar until such time when a "leap month" is added to the Jewish calendar in order to make up for the time lapse.

Jews number the years starting not with the birth of Jesus, but with the Creation. The computation of that event was arrived at by a Palestinian rabbi of the second century, Rabbi Jose Ben Halfata. There has never been any religious sanction for this arbitrary system of numbering the years, but it became accepted and is still followed today. Thus, in September of 1969, when Jews celebrated Rosh Hashanah, they were ushering in the New Year of 5730.

The Holidays

Looking at the calendar from a seasonal viewpoint, the Jewish festival year looks like this:

Fall:	Rosh Hashanah (New Year)
	Yom Kippur (Day of Atonement)
	Sukkot (Feast of Tabernacles)
	Simhat Torah (Rejoicing in the Law)
Winter:	Hanukkah (Feast of Lights, or Feast of Dedication)
	Fifteenth of Shevat (Jewish Arbor Day)
	Purim (Feast of Lots)
Spring:	Pesach (Passover)
	Shavuot (Pentecost)
Summer:	Ninth of Av (Destruction of Jerusalem and the Temple)

Rather than examine the holidays in detail in the above order, we have grouped them in three categories:

1. The High Holy Days (Rosh Hashanah and Yom Kippur). Also called the Days of Awe, these are the most sacred days in the Jewish calendar, and their observance is almost entirely synagogue-centered.
2. The Three Pilgrim Festivals (Pesach, Sukkot and Shavuot). These, too, are days of primary religious significance, on which major synagogue services are held.
3. Other Holidays (Hanukkah, Purim, Fifteenth of Shevat, Ninth of Av). These, along with a few others are considered "minor" holidays. Of less weight in religious terms, nevertheless the first two in particular—because of their origins in important national events in the life of the Jewish people—have become "major" in terms of the scope of their observance.

The High Holy Days: (Rosh Hashanah and Yom Kippur)

Rosh Hashanah, which in Hebrew means "first of the year," comes in September or October. Observance of the holiday is biblically ordained: "On the first day of the seventh month you shall have a holy convocation; you shall do no laborious work. It is a day for you to blow the Shofar." (Numbers 29: 1-2; Lev. 23:24-25). Rosh Hashanah marks the beginning of the "High Holy Days," or the "Days of Awe." Yom Kippur, the Day of Atonement, which comes ten days after Rosh Hashanah, concludes this holy period.

Orthodox and Conservative synagogues celebrate Rosh Hashanah for two days, in accordance with ancient traditions. Reform congregations observe the holiday for only one day.

Rosh Hashanah is not the kind of jovial, merrymaking New Year that January 1st is, but neither is it a day of sadness. It might rather be characterized as a time of joyous solemnity; a time to reaffirm God's sovereignty, and to praise Him for the creation of the world. And it is a time for soul-searching, and taking stock of one's behavior during the past year.

Repentance, or return to the ways of God, is the basic theme of Rosh Hashanah and of Yom Kippur. Rosh Hashanah is called "the birthday of the world," for it is a day on which, spiritually, life starts anew. Every man is judged, and every man is enabled to repent, to start afresh. These basic concepts are most beautifully expressed in one of the central Rosh Hashanah prayers, *"Un'tah'neh To'kef"*:

"We will observe the mighty holiness of this day; for it is one of awe and anxiety. . . .

"The great *Shofar* is sounded, and a still small voice is heard. The angels in heaven are dismayed and are seized with fear and trembling; as they proclaim, 'Behold the Day of Judgment! . . .'

"But repentance, prayer and righteousness avert the severity of the decree. . . . Thou art slow to anger and ready to forgive. Thou desirest not the death of the sinner but that he return from his evil way and live. Even until his dying day Thou waitest for him, perchance he will repent and Thou wilt straightway receive him. . . ."

The chief symbol of the High Holy Days is the *shofar,* the ram's horn, which was used in biblical times at coronations and other ceremonial occasions. The *shofar* is blown at four key points of the Rosh Hashanah service, and to signal the conclusion of Yom Kippur. The piercing notes are meant to evoke specific spiritual or historical associations: the celebration of God's kingship, "remembrance" of God's concern for man throughout history and the evocation of all those events past and future (the giving of the Torah at Sinai, the coming of the Messianic Age) which the Bible has linked with the blowing of the *shofar.*

Over the centuries, many colorful customs have become part of Rosh Hashanah:

Worshipers greet each other and their families with the blessing *"L'Shanah Tovah Tikatayvu.* . . . May you be inscribed for a good year." Greetings cards bearing this or a similar blessing are exchanged.

During meals on Rosh Hashanah pieces of apple sweetened in honey are eaten, accompanied by the prayer, "May it be Thy will that a good and a sweet year be renewed for us."

The *tashlich* ceremony, echoing the biblical scapegoat ritual, originated in the 15th century, and is still adhered to by some traditional Jews. It consists of going to a body of water on the first afternoon of Rosh Hashanah and reciting the verses of Micah 7:18-20, which include the words, "And Thou wilt cast all their sins into the depths of the sea."

Yom Kippur: The Day of Atonement

Yom Kippur is the "Sabbath of Sabbaths"—the holiest day in the Jewish calendar. It consists of a twenty-four-hour period completely given over to confession of sins, remorse over wrongdoing and a search for reconciliation and forgiveness, during which time Jews abstain from food and work. It also culminates the ten-day repentance period.

The biblical Yom Kippur was an observance involving sacrificial rites in which the High Priest played the major role (Lev. 16:29-32). In the post-biblical Rabbinic period (200 B.C.E.-500 C.E.), Yom Kippur, no longer revolving solely around the High Priesthood and the sacrificial system, lost none of its awesomeness. The Prophets had maintained that where there was no repentance, sacrifice availed nothing. Thus, when sacrifice ended, true repentance was the sole means of the remission of sins.

Like all Jewish holidays, Yom Kippur begins at sundown of the previous day. Prior to the beginning of the fasting period, the entire family eat a festive meal to indicate that the fasting is approached, not in a spirit of doom, but with an eager anticipation of God's grace.

The *Kol Nidre* Service (*Kol Nidre* means "All Vows"), which is recited on the eve of Yom Kippur, is the most impressive service of the day. The plaintive melody of this traditional prayer, with its echoes of the Crusades, the Inquisition and the numberless other calamities the Jews have suffered, infuses every worshiper with a sense of the solemnity of this occasion when man faces his Maker to ask forgiveness for past errors and for help in facing the future. The last words of the day's services—after the final blowing of the *shofar* are "Next year in Jerusalem." Thus is expressed the hope that one day all Jews will be reunited as of old.

The fundamental mood of the Day of Atonement is distilled in the Hebrew word *teshuvah,* ordinarily defined as "repentance" or "penitence." It expresses remorse over misdeeds and implies a change in the sinner's heart and acts.*

The doctrine of repentance is one of the basic pillars upon which the entire edifice of Judaism is built. It implies that, by an act of will, man can free himself from iniquity, mischief and malice—so that the path of his constant renewal and regeneration is fully laid out before him.

The theme of repentance occurs repeatedly in the Bible, particularly in the Prophets. Its meaning is further elucidated in numerous laws, sayings, parables and legends in the Talmud. Here are two brief talmudic selections that capture the simplicity and universality of this concept:

> A king had a son who had gone astray from his father on a journey of a hundred days. His friends said to him, "Return to your father"; he said, "I cannot." Then his father said to say, "Return as far as you can, and I will come to you the rest of the way." So God says, "Return to me, and I will return to you." **
>
> To a man who says, "I will sin and repent," the Day of Atonement brings no forgiveness. For sins against God, the Day of Atonement brings forgiveness; for sins against a man's neighbor, the Day of Atonement bring no forgiveness till a man has become reconciled with his neighbor.***

The Three Festivals

The Feasts of Passover (Pesach), Pentecost (Shavuot) and Tabernacles (Sukkot) were originally celebrations of harvest time, the first two in the spring of the year, the third in the fall. They originated at a time when the children of Israel were primarily an agricultural people. Gradually, historic and religious significance was attached to the purely agricultural aspects of each festival, and the festivals became a kind of annual drama through which the Jews relived the story of how their ancestors became bound in a covenant with God.

The agricultural element has always remained a part of each festival, though outside the Land of Israel it has tended to be more of symbolic than any real importance. On the other hand, in the present State of Israel, where many Jews are farmers once again, actual harvest festivals are celebrated in addition to the synagogue and home rituals. (In ancient

---

Teshuvah is translated into the New Testament as *metanoia,* or "change of mind (and heart)"; it was the "repentance" (Mat 3:2) that John the Baptist, who was probably an Essene, preached.

**This is echoed in Jesus' parable of The Prodigal Son (Lk 15:11-32).

***This, also, is a value in the teaching of Jesus (Mat 5:23).

times, when the center of Jewish religious life was the Temple, Pesach, Shavuot and Sukkot were the occasions for major pilgrimages to Jerusalem, where offerings of thanksgiving were placed on the Temple altar.)

Passover

Passover commemorates the Exodus of the children of Israel from Egypt, where they were enslaved, more than 3,000 years ago. The meaning of that event is reiterated and emphasized throughout the Jewish tradition and in the liturgy, and may be considered to contain its most important teachings. (*See* "What Is Judaism?") The story of the Exodus is set down in the Book of Exodus, chapters 1-15. The significance of their journey from slavery to freedom was so great that they were commanded to retell and to relive it symbolically (Exod. 13:6-10).

The feast and ceremony commemorating the flight from Egypt is called the *Seder*. A joyous occasion, a festive meal and a worship service all at the same time, the *Seder* is celebrated by the family and its guests (often strangers) with prayers, songs and blessings performed in a given order. In fact, *seder* is the Hebrew word for "order."

The *Seder* is held on both the first and second nights of the eight-day holiday. (Reform Jews hold only one *Seder.*) Some synagogues, generally Conservative or Reform, now also conduct a *Seder* for their entire congregation.

The appointed order for the *Seder* ceremonies is contained in the *Haggadah,* an ancient book whose oldest portions date back at least twenty-five hundred years.

Children play a meaningful role in the *Seder* service. In fact, the service opens with the youngest child in the family asking four questions of his father, beginning with the famous *"Ma Nishtanah"* ("Why is this night different from all other nights?"). It is the father's answers that unfold the drama of the Exodus. In addition, children partake actively in the *Seder* in the sense that they join in the singing, are sent to open the door so that Elijah may enter (see below), and are promised a present if they find the *afikomen*—a piece of *matzah* which the father has hidden and is the last thing that one is allowed to eat at the *Seder* table.

Placed on the table at the *Seder* is a large platter containing all the symbolic foods used in the ritual of the evening. As the *Haggadah* is read, and the foods eaten, their meaning is revealed. The *matzah* (unleavened bread) represents the bread the Jews ate on their exodus from Egypt, when they fled with such haste that they could not even wait for the bread to leaven; the *maror,* or bitter herbs, are a reminder of the bitterness of slavery; the *haroset,* the mixture of chopped apples, nuts, cinnamon and wine represents the mortar with which the Jews made the bricks for the Pharaoh's great cities; the lamb shank bone is a reminder of the paschal lamb which was offered as a sacrifice in the Temple of Jerusalem during the spring pilgrimage of the earliest Hebrews; the roasted egg is a symbol of the free-will offering that accompanied the sacrifice of the paschal lamb, and the parsley, lettuce or potato reminds everyone of the continual rebirth of growing things, and is a token of gratitude to God for the products of the earth that come to life each spring.

As in most Jewish ceremonies, wine is a part of the ritual, and a cup of wine is placed at each setting. Also on the table is a goblet of wine called "Elijah's cup." Tradition says that the prophet Elijah will foretell the coming of the Messiah. By filling this cup with wine, Jews welcome his presence at the *Seder,* and thereby express their hope that the promise of a Messianic Age will someday be fulfilled.

The *Seder* is not solely a religious rite. It is also an educational event, a lesson whose aim is to attune the participants to the religious and ethical meaning of the Exodus. This lesson teaches that it was God, not man, who freed the Jews from bondage, and that He did so for two purposes: to give them the Torah at Mount Sinai, and to bring them to the Promised Land.

The ethical teaching of the Exodus may be summarized in this section from the *Haggadah:*

> In each generation, every man is duty-bound to envision himself as though he personally took part in the Exodus from Egypt; as we read in the Torah: 'You shall tell your son on that day, saying, It is because of what the Eternal did for *me* when I came forth from Egypt.' It was not only our forefathers that the Holy One, blessed be He, redeemed; He redeemed us, the living, together with them.

It has become customary at the *Seder* for Jews to recall the terrible sufferings of their people throughout history, particularly during the Nazi era. Today, many Jews leave an empty seat at the table for the Jews in the Soviet Union, and they have brought a more universal dimension to the *Seder* by reading appropriate selections about enslaved peoples everywhere, including the blacks and other minority groups in this country.

The yearning for Zion and Jerusalem is a recurrent theme of the *Seder* service. The *Seder* in fact concludes—as does the Yom Kippur

Service—with the phrase "Next year in Jerusalem," thus expressing the timeless bond of the Jew to Zion.

Influence of Passover on Christianity

Easter was originally called "The Pascha"—and in some sections of Christendom it is still known by this Jewish reference. "The Pascha," or the paschal lamb offered by the ancient Israelites as their annual Passover Eve sacrifice, associates Easter with Pesach. It is believed that the bread to which Jesus referred at the Last Supper was actually *matzah,* since it is presumed to have been a Passover meal eaten in Jerusalem at the time of the festival. Thus, at every Mass, the Jewish Passover is recalled by Roman Catholics, for the bread used as the host—the thin wafer—must always be unleavened.

Shavuot

Seven weeks after the beginning of Passover comes Shavuot, the Feast of Weeks. (It is also called Pentecost—"fifty" in Greek—because it falls on the fiftieth day after Passover.)

First celebrated in biblical days as the conclusion of the grain harvest (Lev. 23:15-22), Shavuot was later identified as the holiday commemorating the revelation of the Ten Commandments to Moses at Sinai. Still more recently, Shavuot has been established by Reform Jews as the day for the holding of confirmation ceremonies.

On Shavuot Eve, many Jews read the Bible and study other religious books all night. The Book of Ruth is also read on this holiday, since it refers to the harvest and tells how Ruth, a non-Jew, embraced Judaism and its commandments. In all synagogues, the Ten Commandments are publicly read at the Shavuot morning services.

One of the loveliest Shavuot customs is the decoration of house and synagogue with "a harvest" of spring plants and flowers.

Sukkot—Tabernacles or the Festival of Booths

Five days after the solemnity of Yom Kippur comes Sukkot, a festival celebrating the fall fruit harvest of ancient Israel. (Lev. 23:35-43) Some scholars believe that the American Pilgrim fathers were inspired to hold their first Thanksgiving by the Sukkot festival about which they had read in the Bible.

During the eight days of this holiday, some Jews eat their meals in a *sukkah,* a little booth or hut with an open roof of branches and leaves. These booths commemorate the temporary shelters in which the ancient

Israelites lived, as they followed Moses on their 40-year journey from Egypt to the Promised Land.

In the past, it was customary for each Jewish family to build its own *sukkah,* but today, it has become more usual for the members of a synagogue to build one large *sukkah* for the entire congregation.

A high point of the Sukkot worship is the daily blessing of the *lulav* (a palm branch to which some sprigs of myrtle and willow are attached) and the *etrog* (a fragrant lemon-like fruit). The service includes prayers of thanksgiving for God's bounty.

The first two days of Sukkot are observed by Orthodox and Conservative Jews as full holidays, with special prayers and biblical readings recited in the synagogue; Reform congregations observe only the first day as a full holiday. The next five days of Sukkot are called *Hol Hamo'ed,* the "week days" of the holiday, which simply means that although special prayers are said in the synagogue on those days, Jewish children and adults may return to their workaday tasks.

It is customary to read from the Book of Ecclesiastes (*Koheleth*) during the *Hol Hamo'ed* period. Like the holiday itself, this book of the Bible reminds us that it is only by trusting in the Lord that man is able to make sense of his life and give it meaning.

The seventh day of Sukkot is observed in some synagogues as Hoshana Rabba (the great hosannas). Accordng to Orthodox tradition, the final judgment of each man by God, begun during the Rosh Hashanah period, is completed on this day. In some synagogues, men, with *lulav* and *etrog* in hand, march around the platform seven times singing hosannas, the prayers for salvation.

The eighth day of Sukkot, called Shemini Atzeret (the eighth day of assembly), is celebrated as a separate festival. An interesting observance of this day is the "Prayer for Rain." Sukkot marks the end of the long dry season in the Holy Land, and the beginning of the hoped-for rains. This was the climate of ancient Israel as it is of modern Israel. Throughout the ages, Jews the world over have always prayed on Sukkot for rain and good crops in the Holy Land.

Simhat Torah

Immediately following Sukkot is Simhat Torah. This holiday arose during the Middle Ages. Simhat Torah means "rejoicing in the Torah," and it marks the completion of the annual cycle of reading the Torah publicly. (See "Aspects of Jewish Theology: Part II.")

On Simhat Torah Eve, a section from the closing chapter of the Book of Deuteronomy, the last part of the Torah, is read aloud. This event is heralded by a procession in which the sacred Scrolls are carried around the synagogue, while the children follow with flags and songs. The next morning another procession takes place and the Scripture reading begins with the last chapter of Deuteronomy and concludes with the first chapter of Genesis.

Simhat Torah demonstrates that the study of God's word is an unending process.

OTHER HOLIDAYS

Hanukkah

In December of every year, Jews observe a festival called Hanukkah, or the Feast of Dedication (see John 10:22). It is a joyous holiday, celebrating the first great victory for religious freedom won by the Jews more than two thousand years ago.

The account of the struggle is recorded in the Books of the Maccabees. In those days (67-163 B.C.E.), the Jews of Palestine were dominated by the rule of Antiochus IV, a Syrian-Greek emperor who demanded that everyone in his empire follow *his* ways of worship. Attempting to force the Jews to adopt his pagan rituals, he seized their Temple in Jerusalem, filled it with idols and then ordered the Jews to abandon their faith on pain of death.

Mattathias, the elder of the town of Modin in Palestine, called on the Jews to revolt. They followed their leader into the hills of Judea where Judah Maccabaeus, one of Mattathias' five sons, organized them into an army. "It is better for us to die in battle than to look upon the tragedies of our nation and sanctuary," he told the Jews. Judah received the name *Maccabaeus*, which means "hammer," because of the blows he struck for freedom.

After fighting for three years Judah Maccabaeus was finally able to lead his troops back to Jerusalem. The story is told that, when Judah's men were cleaning out the Temple, they found just a single jar of holy oil—only enough to keep the Eternal Light before the Holy Ark burning for one day. Miraculously, this one jar burned for eight days and eight nights, allowing the priests of the Temple enough time to prepare a sufficient supply of oil so that the Eternal Light could remain lit without interruption.

Judah Maccabaeus then proclaimed an eight-day holiday to celebrate the rededication of the Temple of God. Thus the festival received its name, for Hanukkah means "dedication."

Children in particular love this holiday, for it has become a time of gifts, games and parties where it is traditional to serve "latkes" (potato pancakes).

Religious observances of the holiday include the candle-lighting ceremony commemorating the light that burned for eight days during the rededication of the Temple. Every night of the festival, the father of the family places candles in a special candelabrum, the Hanukkah *menorah*. In the presence of the whole family he recites special blessings and lights one candle the first night, two the second, and so on until eight candles are lit on the *menorah*.

Fifteenth of Shevat

Tu B'Shevat, the 15th day of the Hebrew month of Shevat, usually falls in February. It is the Jewish Arbor Day, also called the New Year of the Trees. It is not a religious holiday, for there are no special rituals to be observed or prayers to be said. Rather it might be considered a land-related holiday. It originated in ancient Palestine, when Jews celebrated the end of winter by planting new trees.

Throughout the long period of exile, Jews continued to mark this day, affirming the bond with the physical, and not just the spiritual, aspect of the Holy Land. In Israel today, where trees are urgently needed to develop the land, the day is observed with countrywide tree-planting ceremonies. In this country, children in Jewish schools study about Israel's geography and agriculture, and eat some of the fruits that are associated with the Land of Israel—dates, figs, pomegranates, almonds, oranges and the ancient carob (called also St. John's Bread), a dry pod with a sweet pulp that still grows on low trees in the Holy Land.

Purim

The story of Purim is told in the Book of Esther. It commemorates the rescue of Persian Jewry, through the mediation of Esther, from the threat of annihilation engineered by Haman. It is celebrated on the fourteenth day of Adar, which falls in February or March according to our modern calendar.

On Purim Eve, it is traditional to read in the synagogue the Book of Esther (in Hebrew, the *Megillah*). At every mention of Haman's name, the congregation (especially the children) stamp, clap and make noise with their Purim *greggers* (noisemakers). In this fashion, they symbolically blot out Haman's name and the memory of his evil doing. The following morning, special prayers of thanksgiving are recited, expressing gratitude that faith triumphed over hatred and evil.

Purim is celebrated with great gaiety; there are carnivals and parties, costume plays and dances, gifts to the needy and exchange of small gifts to friends and neighbors. The special food of the day is *haman-tashen,* three-cornered pastries filled with jam or poppy seeds.

Although Purim is a day of triumph, the Jews realize—amid all the gaiety—that Haman's defeat was but a temporary one. In every age, they have witnessed how selfish and corrupt men, eager for power, have tried to destroy whatever people or groups stood in their way. In their lust, these dictators have forgotten the Law of God and spread hate and distrust, turning one people against another. Purim is a happy reminder, however, that while evil may seem all-powerful at times, it can be defeated if people of good faith work together.

Ninth of Av

Tisha B'Av, the ninth day of the Hebrew month of Av, which falls during the summer, is a fast day on which Jews commemorate the destruction of Jerusalem and the Holy Temple. Twice on the same date, in 586 B.C.E. by the Babylonians, and in 70 C.E. by the Romans, the Holy City was sacked and the Temple razed. Only the outer Western Wall (later called the Wailing Wall by non-Jews because Jews would cry when visiting it) remained.

The Ninth of Av is the culmination of a three-week period of "national mourning," in which weddings are not permitted by Orthodox and Conservative Jews, and other expressions of joy are curtailed. On Tisha B'Av itself, the Book of Lamentations is read in the synagogue, and traditional Jews abstain from food and drink for 24 hours.

Suggested Classroom Activities and Discussion Topics

This material is suitable for use—with occasional modification—by Catholic, Protestant and Jewish groups.

1. Have the class visit a synagogue. Before the visit, find out whether the synagogue is Orthodox, Conservative or Reform, and try to learn as much as possible about synagogues in general, the general structure of the service and whatever else seems relevant. (Some of the suggested activities that follow might in fact be used as research projects prior to the visit.) If practicable, arrange to have this visit coincide with some religious service, so that the class can get an idea of what it is like.

2. Bring into class copies of various Jewish prayerbooks *see* Bibliography. Have the class note division into daily, Sabbath and Festival services, and take time to read aloud prayers of especial interest, such as the *Shema* ("Hear O Israel, the Lord Our God, the Lord is One"), the *Shemoneh Esrei* (the Standing Prayer) and the *Aleinu* (Adoration). In looking over the prayers, students should note that *personal* petition is almost completely lacking, and that the emphasis is rather on extolling God and on asking for the well-being of all the people of Israel. What, if anything, does this tell you about the Jewish religion?

3. Define, describe, illustrate and discuss the adornments worn during prayer (*tallit,* phylacteries, skullcap) and religious objects in the synagogue (Ark, Torah Scrolls, Eternal Light, menorahs). Note also symbols used in decoration and discuss their origins: e.g. Star of David, Lion of Judah, stone tablets, Burning Bush. Why is there comparatively little art displayed in synagogues (never any sculpture, for example)?

4. In conjunction with a study of ceremonial objects, including those used in home rituals for Sabbath and festivals, have the class visit a Jewish museum if one is readily available (e.g. the Jewish Museum in New York or the Museum of the Hebrew Union College in Cincinnati). Many synagogues throughout the country also have displays of ceremonial objects.

5. *The Torah:* What is it? Why does the reading of the Torah play such a central role in Jewish public worship? If a visit is arranged to a synagogue service, have the class note the way in which the rabbi's sermon makes use of the day's Torah portion.

   How does the rabbi arrive at his interpretation? Do you think a congregant may offer a different interpretation? Draw comparisons with the use of the "homily" in the Catholic Liturgy of the Word.

   Visit a Jewish scribe and observe the copying of Scripture.

6. Have the students compare the three daily services in the synagogue with the Divine Office.

7. In many American synagogues, worship is conducted both in Hebrew and in English. What role has the Hebrew language played historically in Jewish worship? Why do Jews retain Hebrew in their prayers, rather than praying entirely in English? Can a comparison be made with the use of Latin vs. the vernacular in the Catholic

religion? Are there any Hebrew words in the Catholic Missal, or Protestant worship service? (Amen, Selah, Hallelujah, Hosannah, etc.)

8. Set up a committee and assign them the task of comparing and contrasting the training, the role and the duties of the Catholic priest and the rabbi.

9. In Judaism, private prayer or meditation is permitted, but public worship is preferred. What are the reasons for this? Discuss the pros and cons of public and private worship from the students' own personal point of view. What is the Catholic attitude? Protestant?

10. In very large measure the synagogue reflects "participatory democracy," or certainly approaches it. Assign a group of students to find out how the individual synagogue is operated, how decisions are made and by whom. How much authority does the rabbi have? Who makes decisions for all the synagogues, or all those of a particular denomination or trend? This can be followed by class reports and discussions. Another possibility is to discuss the movement within the Church for greater worshipper participation in particular, and for participatory democracy in general.

11. *The Sabbath:* Suggest that students attend a Sabbath service (preferably a junior congregation) with a Jewish friend, or else visit his home on a Friday evening. An "impressionistic" report of the visit could be submitted afterward to the teacher or class.

12. Arrange a "model" Friday evening home service for the class, including perhaps a meal of Jewish foods. The cooperation—and, if possible, the participation—of a local Jewish rabbi, should be enlisted.

13. Compare and contrast Jewish and Christian Sabbath observance. Make note of the individual differences in observance among the various trends in Judaism.

14. Have a group or committee list all the Jewish holidays beginning with the Jewish New Year, and then draw up a comparable list of Catholic and Protestant feasts. Let the class first draw any conclusions it can about similarities or differences—and then carry out research to test theories.

15. The Jewish New Year is approached by observant Jews with thoughts of God's sovereignty and providence, repentance, prayer and a resolve to do justice. Does the class think this is a fitting

way to usher in a new year? Why? How does this compare with the way we celebrate the new year on January 1?

On Rosh Hashanah the traditional greeting is, "May you be inscribed for a good year." On January 1 we say "Happy New Year." What difference, if any, is implied by the phrasing of these greetings?

Someone has said that every man writes his own epitaph. How does each of us add to or detract from our being inscribed for a good year?

16. The High Holy Days are solemn but not sad days. They do not commemorate any tragic event of the past, but are days set aside for introspection and soul-searching. What qualities and characteristics do the Jewish High Holy Days have in common with the Christian Lenten season? Why are contrition and penitence essential to Judaism and Christianity? Compare and contrast Jewish and Christian views of repentance, sin and the moral strength of man.

Read a prayer from one of the High Holy Day Prayer Books and ask the students how it reflects the particular holiday. Note especially the "group confessionals"—"we have sinned."

17. Ask students to compose short prayers that could be said by young Jewish people as well as by themselves expressing the following central ideas: repentance; hope; confession of past misdeeds; request for forgiveness; concern about the state of the world.

18. Assign students to read the Book of Jonah, which is read in the synagogue on Yom Kippur. Have episodes that point up its moral lessons dramatized in class. Discuss the possible reasons for including Book of Jonah in the worship service of the Day of Atonement. Why is it still a popular story today?

19. Show how the biblical story of the Exodus is reflected in the observance of Pesach, Shavuot and Sukkot. What is the historical significance of each festival? What is the religious meaning? List the holidays with both meanings side by side.

20. At the Passover *Seder,* each participant is instructed to consider himself as having been an actual participant in the Exodus from Egypt, as having actually gone from slavery to freedom. What do you think is the purpose of this? Assuming that you can project yourself back into the past to some similar situation or event in the life of your own people, or of the American nation, what effect might that have on your feelings and attitudes? (In this con-

nection, it might be well to remember that people who have gone from "rags to riches" are often admonished to "remember their lowly origins"—which they might actually prefer to forget!) What function can be served by such a "remembering?"

21. Discuss the various kinds of slavery—physical, spiritual, economic, cultural, political—and relate them to particular peoples or countries in the world today. What have been some of the different reactions to, and results of, slavery—both in terms of the oppressors as well as of the victims?

22. Have students write a poem, story or playlet that retells the story of the Exodus, or that uses it as a springboard for dealing with the theme of "from slavery to freedom" in a modern context. (See previous question.)

23. Appoint a committee and assign them the topic of relating Negro spirituals to the Passover story. Are there parallels to be drawn between the experience of the ancient Jews in Egypt and the story of the black people in this country?

24. Make plans for students to attend a *Seder*—either in a private home, or a "model" *Seder* at a synagogue school. (If neither of these are possible, arrange a "model" *Seder* for the class. See No. 12 above.)

25. Relate the Passover Seder to the Last Supper and/or to the Eucharist. This can be either a discussion topic or the subject for an essay.

26. Hanukkah celebrates the victory of the weak over the strong, the few over the mighty. In class discussion, pinpoint this theme in the story of Hanukkah, and then relate it to similar events in the past or in the present.

27. Martyrdom is another important theme in the Hanukkah observance (for example, Hannah and her seven sons). Define "martyr." What is your attitude to martyrs, in general? To the martyrs of the Church? Would you consider as martyrs the Vietnamese Buddhist monks or the Czech students who burned themselves alive? Do the Reverend Martin Luther King, Jr. and Robert Kennedy qualify?

28. Many Jews celebrate Christmas as a "secular" holiday—that is, without participating in any of the religious rituals, but by putting up a tree, exchanging gifts and cards, and so forth. Why do you

think they do this? How do you, as a Christian, feel about it? Is there anything, in this connection, that Christians "borrow" from Jews? If not, why?

29. *An individual or group project:* Write a series of newspaper articles and editorials describing the events of the Hanukkah story (starting, perhaps, with the erection of an idol in the town square of Modin, and concluding with the miracle of the oil found in the Temple).

30. Is religious freedom basic to American democracy? Why?

31. The assertion of God's holiness is a central feature of Jewish worship; it is equally important in Christian liturgy. Yet holiness is not an easy concept to define, even though Judaism is quite specific in what it means by that word (see Leviticus, Chapter 19). What *does* holiness mean to the Jew? to the Christian? Trace its appearance in rituals connected with marriage, death, the dietary laws, the holidays, etc.

32. Compare and contrast the functions and role of the rabbi and the priest.

33. Play for the class a recording of Jewish cantillation—specifically a reading from the prophets, or a reading from the Torah. See "Additional Resources."

Bibliography

The following is a selected listing of books and other resource material that are recommended for a study of Jewish worship and the Jewish holidays. For a more comprehensive bibliography, the teacher may wish to send for *A Bibliography on Judaism and Jewish-Christian Relations,* published by the Anti-Defamation League of B'nai B'rith, 315 Lexington Avenue, New York, N. Y. 10016 (price: $1.00).

1—indicates books suggested for the average high-school student.
2—indicates books suggested for the superior high-school student.
3—indicates books suggested for the average teacher.
4—indicates books suggested for the advanced reader.

Jewish Prayer

3 Hertz, J. H., editor. *The Authorized Daily Prayer Book* (rev. ed.). London: Shapiro, Vallentine and Co., 1959.

The traditional prayerbook, with a fine English translation and a popular commentary. Used by many Orthodox congregations.

3 *Rabbinical Assembly Prayer Book*. New York: Rabbinical Assembly of America, 1953.

The authorized prayerbook of the Conservative trend. Contains a valuable introduction on the relationship of tradition to change.

3 *Union Prayer Book* 2 volumes. New York: Union of American Hebrew Congregations, 1945.

The authorized prayer book of Reform Judaism.

3 Arzt, M. *Justice and Mercy: Commentary on the Liturgy of the New Year and the Day of Atonement*. New York: Holt, Rinehart and Winston, 1963. (Also in paperback.)

A modern commentary, lucidly presented, on the liturgy of the High Holy Days.

2 Arian, P. and Eisenberg, A. *The Story of the Prayer Book*. Hartford, Conn.: Prayer Book Press, 1968.

This book offers more than its title indicates. In the course of describing the development of Jewish prayer through the ages, the authors present a most interesting and readable version of Jewish history—including many colorful legends.

Holidays

2 Gaster, T. H. *Festivals of the Jewish Year: A Modern Interpretation and Guide*. Gloucester, Mass.: Peter Smith, 1962. (Also in paperback.)

An anthropological study of the Jewish festivals that presents parallel customs and ceremonies of other peoples in an attempt to uncover the universal ideas behind them.

2 Heschel, A. J. *The Sabbath*. Philadelphia and Cleveland: Jewish Publication Society and Meridian, 1964.

A lyrical evocation of the meaning of the Seventh Day.

2 Schauss, H. *Guide to Jewish Holy Days: History and Observance*. New York: Schocken, 1962. (Also in paperback.)

Historical and literary analysis of the development of the major Jewish festivals. An authoritative study.

1 Levi, S. B. and Kaplan, S. R. *Across the Threshold: Guide for the Jewish Homemaker*. New York: Schocken. (Also in paperback.)

This popular book, written for Jewish women, explains the holiday rituals and customs (particularly those of the home) in a manner that will be interesting to students. The book will prove particularly helpful if the class intends to prepare any "demonstration" celebrations.

Pamphlets (All ADL publications)

1 Gilbert, A. and Tarcov, O. *Your Neighbor Celebrates.* 40 pp., 35¢. Clear and concise explanations of the major Jewish holidays. Also available in a hardcover edition, with 42 full-page photographs. ($2.50)

1 Gilbert, A. *Your Neighbor Worships.* 32 pp. 50¢. A tour of the synagogue, explaining its history, architecture, ceremonial objects and worship services.

2 Bernards, S. S., editor. *The Living Heritage of the High Holy Days.* From the liturgy of the High Holy Day prayer book, Rabbi Bernards interprets the quality and meaning of Rosh Hashanah and Yom Kippur. Also contains discussion guide and project suggestions. 32 pp. 25¢.

1 Bernards, S. S., editor. *The Living Heritage of Passover: With an Abridged Passover Haggadah in English.* 40 pp. 50¢. An exposition and analysis of the holiday, the symbolism and order of service for the Passover ritual, the Seder, is contained in the Haggadah.

2 Greenberg, D. and Bernards, S. S. *The Living Heritage of Hanukkah.* 47 pp. 50¢. An illustrated booklet on the holiday and the many meanings it has had through the ages. Includes source material; observances and customs; suggestions for class, church and community use; and a bibliography.

Kit of Religious Articles

Contains religious and ceremonial items (some in miniature) used in Jewish worship, copies of the *Passover Haggadah, The Sabbath, Your Neighbor Celebrates, Your Neighbor Worships* as well as a comprehensive, illustrated Instruction Guide. ($10.00)

Note: The materials listed above may be ordered from the Anti-Defamation League of B'nai B'rith, 315 Lexington Avenue, New York, N. Y. 10016.

THE LIFE OF THE JEW

Aims and Objectives

1. To examine the basic life rituals of Judaism, their significance and forms of observance.
2. To compare and contrast the Jewish and Catholic or Protestant beliefs about the sacramental nature of these life rituals.
3. To point out that sacred events in Jewish life may take place elsewhere than in the synagogue.
4. To examine the development of "family" and "education" as basic Jewish values.
5. To note the emphasis given to the Land of Israel and to the Jewish people in the various life rituals.
6. To compare and contrast Jewish and Christian attitudes toward marriage.
7. To illustrate the content of the Dietary Laws and their significance to Jews.
8. To examine the nature of religious observance in the traditional Jewish home.
9. To consider the concept of *mitzvah* as a means of sanctifying daily life.

Overview

This section deals with those events in the life of man that Judaism considers important and sacred, and for which it has established rituals. In these significant moments of a man's life, Jews, like others, feel moved to invoke God's presence and to pray for His blessings and love. For Jews, these ritual milestones are also viewed as occasions for reaffirming the unity of the Jewish people and God's role in the history of this people.*

---

*An interesting characteristic of Judaism emerges from a study of these life rituals, namely, that the synagogue is not the exclusive abode of sanctity, and that the home, too, is holy—as is, in fact, any place where Jews gather for a sacred purpose, or to utter prayers and benedictions. In fact, it has been said that to the English a man's home is his castle, while to the Jew it is his sanctuary.

Throughout these pages we will refer to the film lecture most relevant to this topic, "The Life Cycle of the Jew," by Rabbi Jules Harlow. In his presentation, Rabbi Harlow establishes the theme of "Torah, marriage and good deeds" as the basic and constant thread that runs through the life of a Jew. We will see in the following pages that this theme occurs and reoccurs, with varying emphasis, in the major rituals from birth to death.

Particular attention will be paid to two primary values of Judaism that can be clearly seen when we study the life cycle of a Jew. These are Family ("Marriage") and Education ("Torah"). Since, in the popular mind, Jews have long been known to stress these values, this section provides a natural opportunity for teacher and student to look into the origins and meaning of these elements in the Jewish tradition.

Finally, we will take up the subject of the Dietary Laws (*Kashrut*), which are a central feature of Jewish ritual observance—especially in the home.

Brit (*Ritual Circumcision*)

The rite of circumcision (symbolizing the covenant between God and Abraham) confers no special status on the new-born child. What makes the child "Jewish" is his being born of a Jewish mother—and this applies, even if he is *not* circumcised.

Nor is there any notion of sacrament in *brit* or in any other event of the Jewish life cycle. *This point must be emphasized.* Belief in the Incarnation leads Catholics to the view that God works in a saving way through Christ and Christ's actions, or sacraments. In Judaism, however, there is no intermediary in God's dealing with Israel, and the rituals of the life cycle do not in any sense bring about the kind of "interior change" that occurs through the Catholic sacraments. It may be helpful at this point to note that all of the major rituals of Judaism may be performed without the presence of a rabbi. A marriage, for example, may be solemnized—according to Jewish law—by any "learned and pious" man. This is in obvious contrast to most Catholic sacraments which require the presence of an ordained priest. Still another point to consider in this regard is that, where Catholic teachers tend to see "sacraments" in the Jewish Bible as forerunners of the seven Catholic sacraments, Jews do not.

Note too that circumcision can take place at home, in the hospital or in the synagogue. Family and friends are invited, and it is customary to follow the ceremony with some refreshments and the recital of appropriate benedictions.

Among Reform Jews, the circumcision is frequently performed by a surgeon in the hospital, rather than by a *mohel* (see *"Life Cycle of a Jew"*).*

Pidyon Ha-ben (Redemption of the Firstborn)

The origin of this ritual, which is described by Rabbi Harlow, is Exodus 13:1-16. The Pentateuchal verse is cited, in fact, in Luke 2:22-24, which describes the journey to Jerusalem for the redemption of Jesus.

"Redemption of the Firstborn" is practiced today by Orthodox and many Conservative Jews, but *not* by Reform Jews.

Bar Mitzvah, Bat Mitzvah, Confirmation

Although the fact of becoming a Bar Mitzvah (reaching one's religious majority) is mentioned in the Mishnah, the ceremony of Bar Mitzvah was introduced into Jewish life more than six hundred years ago—which, in Jewish historical terms, means that it is relatively new.

There is no sacramental element involved in Bar Mitzvah; even if the boy does not observe the customary rituals, the mere fact of his becoming thirteen assures him of "adult" status in the Jewish community.

The ceremony of Bat Mitzvah ("daughter of the commandment") was created in this country by Conservative Jews and is not observed in most other countries. Traditional Judaism considered the synagogue and its rituals the province of man, and the home the province of women (though not exclusively so). Modern women, however, have demanded a greater voice in the synagogue, and the Bat Mitzvah ceremony is an expression of this new participation.

The Confirmation ritual is also an American innovation, one that is mostly practiced by Reform and Conservative congregations, as well as by a few Orthodox ones. The ceremony usually takes place on the festival of Shavuot, which commemorates the giving of the Torah at Mount Sinai. In this way, study in religious school is meaningfully linked with the Torah, the cornerstone of Judaism.

Marriage

As Rabbi Harlow indicates, along with the study of Torah and the performance of good deeds, marriage is considered a sacred duty and

---

*The teacher will recall that in previous times Jesus' circumcision (Luke 2:21) was celebrated on New Year's Day.

one of the most important aspects of life. The Rabbis taught that the very first commandment in the Bible, "Be fruitful and multiply" (Gen. 1:28), related to marriage, and they therefore considered it a sin not to marry.

Orthodox and Conservative marriage ceremonies tend to follow the description given by Rabbi Harlow—though among the extreme Orthodox groups the ceremony may be much more elaborate. Many Reform Jews dispense altogether with the *hupah* (the canopy), and in place of the traditional *ketubah* use a more modern "marriage certificate."

Divorce

Traditional Judaism considered divorce to be as much a religious concern as was marriage, and there is extant a huge body of Jewish law on both subjects. The religious procedure for granting divorce is derived from Deuteronomy 24, and it is followed to this day by Orthodox and Conservative Jews (who first obtain a civil divorce). Reform Jews, on the other hand, consider divorce to be *solely* a matter of civil law.

A Jewish divorce is granted if there is the consent of both husband and wife. If mutual consent is lacking, Jewish law provides a number of grounds on which a rabbinic court may decide to grant a divorce— one of these being the refusal of one of the marriage partners to engage in sexual relations.

Death

Rabbi Harlow describes the Jewish rituals of burial, emphasizing the stress placed on simplicity, and the mourning observances that surround death. (Note particularly the emphasis he gives to the meaning of *Kaddish.*) Of especial interest is *Shivah,* which has very important religious, social and human implications, and is characteristically Jewish. (see Classroom Activity No. 4)

Home and Family

In keeping with the Jewish belief that everything in life is or can be sacred, the home is considered a "miniature sanctuary." Judaism has ordained many practices and rituals to be carried out within the home —not just a few times a year, or once a week, but every day. An Orthodox Jew often says one or all of his three daily prayer services at home; he and his family recite benedictions before and after each meal; and, since his wife attends to the preparation of meals according to the

Dietary Laws, she is at the same time performing religious duties (*see* below). Sabbaths and holidays likewise abound with ritual observances in the home (i.e., festive meals, and the singing of songs—both religious and folk—around the dining table).*

Numerous "ceremonial" objects may be found in Jewish homes. They relate to specific holiday or Sabbath observances (e.g., a silver wine goblet for *kiddush;* a *menorah,* or candelabrum, for Hanukkah). Because they are used for religious purposes, they are venerated and loved, but they have no sacramental powers and are not considered "holy" objects.

The one ritual object found in the home that has no specific connection with a celebration is the *mezuzah* (See "Life Cycle of a Jew" and "Jewish Worship"). It is not a "good-luck" charm, as some think, but a symbol and reminder, in Rabbi Harlow's words, of "the quality of life" that Jews are bidden and expected to maintain. This special quality of life that should be exemplified by the Jewish home has to do with the performance of "good deeds"—the third element in the theme of Jewish life. (See the section on *Mitzvah* in "What Jews Believe.")

All the above aspects of Jewish family life—the elevation of marriage and child-rearing to the status of important religious duties, the round of ritual observances assigned to the home, and the emphasis on the performance of "good deeds"—have served to build strong, home-centered Jewish families. Even among non-religious Jews, home life has always been a central value.

Education

At the beginning of his presentation, Rabbi Harlow stresses the centrality of Torah in Jewish life. For this reason, one of the parental hopes for a newborn is that he will both study and observe Jewish teachings throughout his life.

The Bar Mitzvah, Bat Mitzvah and Confirmation ceremonies point up this preoccupation with study. This preoccupation is likewise symbolized by the fact that the synagogue of old was called *Bet Hamidrash,* the "House of Study," and that every modern American synagogue has a religious school as one of its major branches.

Rabbi Harlow also points out that Jewish tradition never intended Bar Mitzvah to be the conclusion of one's Jewish education; on the contrary, education is viewed as a never-ending process. But, since

---

*One sees fewer daily rituals practiced in the homes of Conservative and Reform Jews—but the Sabbath and holidays are fully celebrated there, as Rabbi Harlow notes.

many boys tend to cease their Jewish education at thirteen, the community makes great efforts to encourage its continuation—in high school, in college and in adult education programs.

Today Jewish emphasis on "education" has extended well beyond the confines of "Torah," so that Jews now tend to stress the value of education generally. There are many reasons for this, some of which have been mentioned here. Others are discussed in Part I of this guide, "The American Jew."

Dietary Laws

Traditionally, the Dietary Laws (*Kashrut*) have been an important feature of Jewish life, both inside and outside the home. In his presentation, Rabbi Harlow outlines briefly the main rules for "keeping kosher." More details of this important and well-known practice can be found in any basic reference work on Judaism (see Bibliography at end of this section, and at end of Part II, "What Jews Believe").

Many people have tried to "explain" the rules of *Kashrut* as originating in the ancient need for hygienic precautions, but this "apologetic," rationalized approach is repudiated by most scholars and *Kashrut*-observers. The rabbinic view has traditionally been that a Jew observes the Dietary Laws because God so commanded; in other words, this observance is a discipline, and is intended to promote a spirit of holiness.* The resultant "self-control" is also seen as an important virtue that is inculcated through the practice of the Dietary Laws.

In general, one can say that the Dietary Laws sanctify the act of eating, may serve to heighten the observer's awareness that God is the source of food, and indicate that as humans we are capable of both discernment and discipline.

Strict adherence to the Dietary Laws is practiced today by Orthodox Jews and by some Conservative Jews. Most of the latter practice a modified form of *Kashrut*—i.e., they are likely to accept the general principles and values, but may feel that observing "the letter of the law" is not essential. Reform Judaism has basically rejected the Dietary Laws on the grounds that they do not promote a spiritual attitude and that they are incompatible and inconsistent with modern life. However, some Reform Jews (and secular ones, too) do refrain from eating pork or pork products—perhaps out of some sense of identification with other religious Jews.

---

*See Leviticus, 11:44, 45.

Suggested Classroom Activities and Discussion Topics

These activities can be used—with occasional modification—by Catholic, Protestant and Jewish groups.

1. Have the class describe and explain each of the following life rituals, its meaning for Jews and how it is observed: *Brit,* "Naming of a Girl," Bar Mitzvah, Confirmation, Wedding, Funeral. Are these observances in any way comparable to the Catholic sacraments? to Protestant? How do they differ?

2. When a baby is born, Jews express the wish that the child will grow up "to a life of Torah, marriage and good deeds." Explain what is meant by each of these three terms, and why each is considered so fundamental to Judaism. Are there life rituals that the Catholic and Protestant churches attach equal importance to?

3. Have students write reports comparing Jewish and Catholic attitudes, practices and beliefs toward each of the following: Birth, Marriage (including Divorce), Death.

4. "Sitting *Shivah*" is one of the most important rituals that surround death and relate to the immediate family of the deceased. Many people, among them Sigmund Freud, who wrote a brilliant essay on its importance in helping people come to terms with the loss of a loved one, have held that *Shivah* not only has considerable religious, but other significance as well. What religious purposes does it serve? Human? Social? Compare and contrast it with the Irish wake, family and communal reaction toward death in the Far East, etc.

5. A visit to the Jewish Museum in New York (or places of equivalent interest in other parts of the country) may be arranged, so that the class can see collections of Jewish ceremonial objects from many lands and different periods of history. (Many synagogues have their own smaller collections.)

6. The courtship and marriage customs of various peoples in different periods of history is a fascinating subject. In connection with a study of Jewish marriage, assign a committee to read Part Three, "Courtship and Marriage," in *The Lifetime of a Jew* by H. Schauss (see Bibliography). Another group might be assigned to report

on wedding customs of Jews in the United States in such widely different groups as the Hassidim and Reform Jews.

Compare and contrast these customs with those of Catholics. Are there any conclusions to be drawn from this?

7. Rabbi Harlow cites the historical fact that betrothal and marriage were once separated in time. Have students analyze Matthew 1:18-25 to find an example of this. Why was Joseph in a dilemma over the fact of Mary's pregnancy? (This topic may be linked to project #6, above.)

8. Marriage, family and home are clearly affirmed values for most Jews; celibacy, however, is not held to be an ideal. Have students trace the possible historical reasons for these attitudes. At the same time, it should be pointed out that other religions besides Christianity see some worth in a special celibate vocation—witness Buddhist monks. Since this whole question has become an increasing source of contention within the Church, a discussion of the various views will be both contemporary and meaningful.

9. Jews have traditionally opposed marriage to a member of another faith, unless that person converted to Judaism. Have students carry out research and then report back to the class on the subject of "Conversion to Judaism"—i.e., the Jewish attitude to conversion, and the requirements.

10. Judaism places more stress on "good deeds" than on faith; Martin Luther emphasized that faith alone saves a man; St. Paul wrote that faith without good works is dead. Let students sort out and analyze these different emphases in classroom discussion. Some prior research on what prompted each of these attitudes will help the class to see the extent of the differences.

11. Jewish dietary laws seem incongruous, out-of-date and mechanical to many non-Jews. If possible, assign students to interview Jewish persons who observe the "kosher" prescriptions—to find out what these are about, and why they are observed. Or, since Catholic youngsters often work in Jewish food stores, it should be practicable to have them find out as much as they can about the observance of *Kashrut*. What do the students consider to be from their point of view the positive and negative aspects of observing these laws? Discuss.

12. Assign students to find out: (1) what Jewish educational facilities

are available in their community or near the school; (2) what form of education their Jewish friends receive. Have them compare their own religious training with that of Jewish students.

13. The Friday night, or Sabbath Eve home service, is one of the most beautiful rituals in Judaism. *See* the "Suggested Classroom Activities" at the end of Section III, "Jewish Worship and the Jewish Year," for ideas on a project revolving around the Friday evening ritual and other home observances.

14. Students may well know Jewish boys and girls who are becoming Bar or Bat Mitzvah, or being confirmed. Ask those who do to learn all they can about these observances (if possible let them attend the actual ceremonies), and then report back to the class with their findings. An interesting discussion might revolve around the similarities and differences between Catholic Confirmation and the Jewish observances of Bat Mitzvah, Bar Mitzvah and Confirmation.

15. A class showing of the film "The Life Cycle of a Jew," the script of which is included in this guide. (This and other films are available through the Audio-Visual Department of the ADL.) Following the film, some of the discussion questions listed here may be very profitably utilized. In addition, the film will serve both as background and springboard for treating the entire subject.

Bibliography

The following is a selected listing of books and other resource material, mostly from Jewish sources, that will prove helpful for a study of the Jewish religion. For a more comprehensive bibliography, the teacher may wish to send for *A Bibliography on Judaism and Jewish-Christian Relations*, published by the Anti-Defamation League, 315 Lexington Ave., New York, N. Y. 10016 (Price: $1.00).

1—indicates books suggested for the average high-school student.
2—indicates books suggested for the superior high-school student.
3—indicates books suggested for the average teacher.
4—indicates books suggested for the advanced reader.

The Life of the Jew

3 Dresner, S. H. and Seigel, S. *The Jewish Dietary Laws.* New York: Burning Bush Press, 1959.

A 71-page pamphlet containing a clear presentation of the religious ideas embodied in the practice of Dietary Laws, and a concise guide to the laws themselves.

1 Levi, S. B. and Kaplan, S. R. *Guide for the Jewish Homemaker.* New York: Schocken (paperback).

This popular book was written for Jewish women, but its explanations and descriptions of Jewish life events and home observances are fine for students as well. The book will prove especially helpful if the class is planning a demonstration celebration of its own, or a visit to a Jewish home or synagogue.

1 *Sabbath Eve Service for the Home.* Available on cards selling for 10¢ each at the National Federation of Temple Sisterhoods.

2 Schauss, H. *The Lifetime of a Jew.* New York: Union of American Hebrew Congregations, 1950.

A fascinating book—popular, yet based on impeccable scholarship—that describes in vivid detail the life-cycle rituals of Jews in different epochs and lands, from the biblical period to modern times.

2 Wouk, H. *This is My God.* New York: Doubleday and Company, 1959. (Also available in paperback.)

The well-known author of *The Caine Mutiny* looks back at his childhood and early influences, among which his grandfather figures very strongly.

General Reference Works

The books listed in this section are for basic reference. They cover almost all areas of Jewish life. Specialized bibliographies will be found at the end of each section of this guide.

1 — Indicates books suggested for the average high-school student.
2 — Indicates books suggested for the superior high-school student.
3 — Indicates books suggested for the average teacher.
4 — Indicates books suggested for further reading.

1   Ausubel, N., *Book of Jewish Knowledge*. New York: Crown, 1964.

A single-volume, handy encyclopedia containing basic and precise information; a comprehensive digest of Judaica, profusely illustrated.

2   Baron, J. L., editor. *A Treasury of Jewish Quotations*. New York: Crown, 1956.

Guide to aphorisms, maxims and comments of Jewish authorship and/or Jewish themes.

2   Fine, M. and Himmelfarb, M., editors. *American Jewish Year Book*. Philadelphia: American Jewish Committee and Jewish Publication Society (annual publication).

Authoritative compendium of demographic, civic, political, religious and cultural data concerning Jews in the U.S.A. and around the world.

3   Finkelstein, L., editor. *Jews: Their History, Culture, and Religion*. 2 volumes (3rd ed.), New York: Harper & Row, 1960.

An important compendium of essays of leading scholars on Jewish history, religion, sociology and demography and the role of Judaism in civilization. Especially useful are the article "The Jewish Religion," by Dr. Finkelstein, Chancellor of the Jewish Theological Seminary, and the Appendix which lists frequently asked questions about Judaism and refers the reader to the relevant chapters.

3   Flannery, E. H. *Anglish of the Jews: Twenty-Three Centuries of Anti-Semitism.* New York: MacMillan, 1965. (Also in paperback.)

This book, the first written by a Catholic priest on the history of anti-Semitism, traces its development through the period of the early Church, the fall of Rome, the Dark Ages, the Renaissance and into modern times.

2   Grayzel, S. *A History of the Jews.* Philadelphia: Jewish Publication Society, 1947.

Recommended for school libraries, this one-volume work is both authoritative and readable.

4   *The Jewish People: Past and Present;* 4 volumes. New York: Jewish Encyclopedia Handbooks, 1955.

A collection of monographs on Jewish history, religion and literature by leading scholars.

2   Landman, I., editor. *The Universal Jewish Encyclopedia;* 10 volumes. New York: Universal Jewish Encyclopedia Company, 1939-1943. Reprinted by Ktav, 1969.

A popular presentation of Jews and Judaism since the earliest times.

2   Leviant, C., editor. *Masterpieces of Hebrew Literature: A Treasury of 2000 Years of Jewish Creativity;* New York: Ktav, 1969.

An in-depth portrait, covering the major periods from the Apocrypha to the 18th century. Brief introductions place works and authors in perspective.

2   Marcus, J. *The Jew in the Medieval World: A Source Book 315-1791;* New York: Atheneum, 1969 (paperback).

An excellent anthology of source material reflecting the life of the medieval Jew as seen through the eyes of contemporaries. An important reference book.

3   Margolis, M. and Marx A. *History of The Jewish People;* New York: Meridian Books (paperback), 1958.

An acknowledged landmark in Jewish historiography. The history of the Jews up to 1925.

3   Millgram, A. E., editor. *Great Jewish Ideas: God-Torah-Israel.* Washington, D.C.: B'nai B'rith, 1959 (Also in paperback).

What makes Judaism different? What are its key ideas? Answers to these and related subjects can be found in this volume which deals with the uniqueness of Judaism and the specific ideas that differentiate it from other religious faiths.

4 Moore, G. F. *Judaism in The First Centuries of The Christian Era;* 2 volumes. Cambridge: Harvard University, 1950.

> A classic study of the Christian scholar, in which he discusses the religious conceptions and moral principles of Judaism and its modes of worship and observance, in the form in which, by the end of the second century, they attained general acceptance.

3 Noveck, S., editor. *Great Jewish Personalities;* Washington, D.C.: B'nai B'rith, 1959. (Also in paperback.)

> This two-volume collection of essays—the contributions of distinguished scholars—offers an exciting view of 5,000 years of Jewish history through the men who were the participants. Volume I Moses to the Vilna Gaon (18th century), Volume II Moses Mendelssohn to Chaim Weizmann.

3 Noveck, S., editor. *Great Jewish Thinkers of the Twentieth Century— Contemporary Jewish Thought: A Reader.* Washington, D.C.: B'nai B'rith, 1959. (Also in paperback.)

> Volume I is a collection of critical essays on ten key figures in twentieth-century Jewish thought. Some of those included are: Martin Buber, Mordecai M. Kaplan, Leo Baeck, and Joseph B. Soloveitchik. Volume II is a source book of the writings of these men.

3 Pearl, C. and Brooks, R. S. *A Guide to Jewish Knowledge.* London: Jewish Chronicle Publications, 1956.

> A clear, brief guide to the Jewish religion, history and language, with concise bibliography for further study. Excellent for introductory text and quick reference.

2 Roth, C. *The Standard Jewish Encyclopedia* (3rd edition). New York: Doubleday, 1959.

> Concise, up-to-date, one volume encyclopedia. A handy reference book, well illustrated.

2 Schneiderman, H. and Karpmen, I. J. *Who's Who in World Jewry.* New York: David McMay, 1965.

> An important reference book providing biographical data of prominent contemporary Jews throughout the world.

3 Schwarz, L. *Great Ages and Ideas of the Jewish People.* New York: Random House, 1956.

> Essays on the Biblical Age by L. Y. Kaufmann, the Hellenistic Age by R. Marcus, Talmudic Age by G. Cohen, Judeo-Islamic by A.

Halkin, European by C. Roth and Modern by S. Baron. An important collection.

2 Singer, I., managing editor. *The Jewish Encyclopedia;* 12 volumes. New York: Funk and Wagnalls, 1901-1906. Reprinted New York: Ktav Publishing, 1963.

Although it contains no information after 1906, this remains the authoritative encyclopedia on Jews and Judaism.

2 Werblowsky, R. J. and Wigoder, G., editors. *The Encyclopedia of the Jewish Religion.* New York: Holt, Rinehart and Winston, 1966.

An illustrated, one-volume compendium of brief, easily readable articles—with numerous cross-references—devoted solely to the Jewish religion. Excellent for school libararies.

There are two excellent general sources that should be found in any good Catholic high-school library. They are:

The New Catholic Encyclopedia, 15 volumes. New York: McGraw-Hill, 1967.

See: Oesterreicher, J. M. "Judaism," vol. pp. 3-13.

Msgr. Oesterreicher writes about Judaism's birth, seminal ideas and history in the 1st Christian century; Rabbinical Judaism; Jews in modern times and differences in their modern practices; the relationship between Jews and Jesus; the present and future of Jews, and a Christian view of Judaism.

The Index, Volume XV, offers detailed articles on Jewish Art, Liturgy, Philosophy, Post-Biblical History, etc.

The Catholic Encyclopedia for School and Home, 12 volumes. New York: McGraw-Hill, 1965.

See: Silverman, D. W. "Judaism," Vol. VI pp. 78-84.

Rabbi Silverman writes as comprehensively but more simply than Oesterreicher—this second encyclopedia was intended to be so written.

The Index, Volume XII, cites additional articles that are pertinent to Judaism.

Additional Resources

Filmstrips

Baal Shem Tov: The Teachings of Hasidism/66 frames/color/12" LP record/27 minutes/$13.50/Union of American Hebrew Congregations.
　The story of the founder of this pietistic movement which started in the 18th century.

Hillel: Teacher of Love/35 frames/color/$9.50/Union of the American Hebrew Congregations.
　Highlights in the life and teachings of this great figure of inter-testamental times.

Maimonides/44 frames/color/$7.50/Includes narrator's script/Jewish Education Committee of New York.
　Dramatic account of Maimonides, scholar, physician and philosopher of the 12th century who influenced Aquinas.

Queen Esther/42 frames/$2.50/Cathedral Films.
　An effective, entertaining and accurate portrayal of the biblical story of Purim. Simple, direct, non-archaic language.

Rav and Samuel: Teachers of Law/44 frames/color/$7.50/Includes two copies of Teacher's Guide/Union of American Hebrew Congregations.
　Traces the careers of two famous scholars involved in the writing of the Babylonian Talmud. Impressive, informative, intellectually stimulating.

Films

The Book and the Idol/14 1/2 minutes/color/Rental/ADL.
　Traces the historic conflict between monethiseim and paganism as dramatized by archaeological artifacts from Israel's earliest civilization.

If Not Higher/30 minutes/Rental $10/New York Board of Rabbis.
　This dramatic adaptation of classic Yiddish story by I. L. Peretz of mercy and man's love for his fellow man tells of the Tzadik of Nemirov whose disciples believe that he ascends to heaven during the pre-Yom Kippur period and of the skeptic who learns that he goes even higher than that. Highly recommended.

The Innocent Eye of a Man of Galilee: Shalom of Safed/28 minutes/color/Rental/ADL.
　Explores the biblical paintings—exquisite, innocent and delightful—of Shalom of Safed, the 70-plus year old Hasid, native of the Galilean town.

Israel the Reality/28 minutes/Rental/ADL.
Israel's land and people as seen by still photographers over the past 50 years. Features work by a Christian doctor, a German Jew and an American Jew—a photographer for *Life* magazine, killed in the Six Day War.

Israel/28 minutes/Rental/ADL.
The first part shows Jewish history from the time of the Patriachs and is done in animated sequence. The second part uses stills of early re-settlement by Zionists and color photography for the life of Israel today.

Night and Fog/31 minutes/color/Rental $25/The Co-op Film Library at Cardinal Spellman H.S., 1991 Needham Ave., Bronx, N. Y. 10466. (212) 881-8000-Ext. 45.
Renais' classic documentary on man's inhumanity to man: life in the Nazi concentration camps. Recommended for high-school seniors or older.

The Image of the Jews consists of two unique film series produced as a jointly sponsored project of the Archdiocese of New York and the Anti-Defamation League of B'nai B'rith. All films are in black and white and cleared for TV.

Series I: Jews and Their Religion (30 minutes each)

Who Are the American Jews? *Dore Schary*
Surveys the development of the American Jewish community, its participation in community affairs, its concern with philanthropy and human relations work, and its relationship to the State of Israel.

What is Judaism? *Rabbi Irving Greenberg*
An historical-religious essay on Judaism's attitude and response to life and the world; the meaning of Jewish law and its central role in Jewish life throughout history and the contemporary challenge.

The Life Cycle of the Jew. *Rabbi Jules Harlow*
Jewish moral and ethical values and how they are reflected in the ceremonies and rituals related to birth, circumcision, religious education, bar mitzvah, marriage and family, divorce, illness, old age and death.

Jews and Their Worship. *Rabbi Max J. Routtenberg, Cantor Ben Belfer*
The basic elements and aspects of Jewish prayers and synagogue worship are described and analyzed. By way of example, selections from the liturgical service are chanted.

Judaism: Orthodox, Conservative, Reform. *Dr. Michael Wyschogrod*
A description of variant practices within Judaism, their theological and historical roots and an examination of the significance of these divisions for contemporary Jewish life. The basic unity underlying all sections of the Jewish community—including the non-observant—is also dealt with.

Aspects of Jewish Theology. *Rabbi Eugene Borowitz*
The first lecture deals with Judaism's definition of God, Hebrew Scriptures, dogma and creed, diversity and unity, God's covenant with mankind and with Israel, and the Jews as an exemplar people.

In the second lecture such topics as the concept of original sin, free will, repentance, Israel, Messianism and the Kingdom of God are discussed. Both programs include readings from the Bible, prayer book, Maimonides, etc.

Series II: The Image of the Jew in Literature

The Jew in the Middle Ages: Evolution of a Stereotype
Two scholars, Rabbi David W. Silverman, Jewish Theological Seminary of America, and Msgr. Eugene V. Clarke, Secretary to the Most Rev. Terence J. Cooke, Archbishop of New York, trace the growth and development of the image of the Jew from the tenth to the fourteenth century and examine some of the historic, cultural, and religious bases for this image. A discussion with two Catholic teachers follows the major presentation.   60 min.

The Jewish Stereotype in English Literature: Shylock and Fagin. *Ilja Wachs*
An analysis of the function and role stereotypes play in life and in literature, with particular reference to the characters in the *Merchant of Venice* and *Oliver Twist*.   30 min.

Panel Discussion: Three Catholic teachers join Prof. Wachs in discussing the implications of his thesis, in evaluating their present methods of teaching these characters, and in suggesting other approaches. 30 min.

The American Jewish Writer. *Louis Zara*
This program traces the American experience of some 20th Century Jewish writers and pays particular attention to three contemporary literary figures— Bernard Malamud, Saul Bellow and Philip Roth.   30 min.

Panel Discussion: Three teachers join Mr. Zara in discussing the works of American Jewish writers and their proper place in the high school English class.   30 min.

Jewish Legends and Tales. *Elie Wiesel*
Elie Wiesel, novelist and master story teller, talks about his own European Hasidic background and his experiences in the "Kingdom of Night" (the Holocaust), illustrating this material with a number of Jewish tales from the Midrash and Hasidic literature.   60 min.

Writings of the Nazi Holocaust. *Ernst Pawel*
A moving and penetrating analysis of holocaust literature with examples from the poetry, fiction, non-fiction and personal journals of Jews as well as non-Jews.   30 min.

Panel Discussion: Dr. Joseph Lichten of the ADL and three teachers discuss the meaning of the Holocaust and how it might be taught.

30 min.

For further information regarding content, rental prices, teachers' guides and special rates for religious institutions, write to:

Audio-Visual Department

ANTI-DEFAMATION LEAGUE
315 Lexington Avenue
New York, N.Y. 10016

or to your nearest ADL regional office.

Recordings

Jewish Folk Songs
Elektra EKL 141 12 in., 33-1/3 rpm. Yiddish folk songs from Eastern Europe sung by Theodore Bikel. Complete text and translation included.

Sephardic Songs
Folkways Records FW8737 12 in., 33-1/3 rpm. Songs of Jews from non-European countries sung by Gloria Levy, with mandolin, drum and guitars.

A Town Hall Concert
Elektra EKL 201 12 in., 33-1/3 rpm. Geula Gill and Oranim-Zabar Troupe sing Israeli songs. Complete text and translation.

The Art of the Cantor. (Vol. 1, 2, 3)
RCA Victor VCM 6173 12 in., 33-1/3 rpm. The late world renowned Cantor Josef Rosenblatt, with choir and instrumentalists.

The Call of the Shofar and Scriptural Cantillations
Folkways FR8922 12 in., 33-1/3 rpm. Recorded by David Hausdroff.

Passover Seder Festival
Columbia ML5736 12 in., 33-1/3 rpm. Richard Tucker, tenor; Ben Irving, narrator; Sholom Secunda, composer and conductor.

Sacred Service (Sabbath Morning)
Columbia ML5621 12 in., 33-1/3 rpm. Sung by Robert Merrill; New York Philharmonic, Leonard Bernstein, Conductor.

Shabbat at Home
Produced by the National Women's League of The United Synagogue of America, 3080 Broadway, New York, N.Y. 10027. Depicts in song, prayer and stories the Sabbath in traditional Jewish homes. Guide book and transliteration included. Especially recommended.

National Jewish Organizations

Additional information on various aspects of Jewish religious and communal life may be obtained from writing to the following national Jewish organizations. (For a complete listing of Jewish organizations see *The American Jewish Yearbook.*)

Community Relations

American Jewish Committee, 165 East 56th Street, New York, N.Y. 10022

American Jewish Congress, 15 East 84th Street, New York, N.Y. 10028

Anti-Defamation League of B'nai B'rith, 315 Lexington Avenue, New York, N.Y. 10016

Research and Education

American Association for Jewish Education, 101 Fifth Avenue, New York, N.Y. 10003

American Jewish Historical Society, 2 Thornton Road, Waltham, Mass. 02154

B'nai B'rith Hillel Foundation, 1640 Rhode Island Avenue, N.W. Washington, D.C. 20036 (For College Groups)

Jewish Book Council of America, 15 East 26th Street, New York, N.Y. 10010

Yivo Institute for Jewish Research, 1048 Fifth Avenue, New York, N.Y. 10028

Philanthropy

American Jewish Joint Distribution Committee, (JDC) 60 East 42nd Street New York, N.Y. 10017

United Jewish Appeal, 1290 Avenue of the Americas, New York, N.Y. 10019

Council of Jewish Federations and Welfare Funds, 315 Park Avenue S. New York, N.Y. 10010

Religious

Jewish Reconstructionist Foundation, 15 West 86th Street, New York, N.Y. 10024

Jewish Theological Seminary of America, (Conservative) 3080 Broadway, New York, N.Y. 10027

Union of American Hebrew Congregations, (Reform) 835 Fifth Avenue, New York, N.Y. 10021

Yeshiva University, (Orthodox) 186 Street and Amsterdam Avenue, New York, N.Y. 10033

Zionist

American Zionist Council, 515 Park Avenue, New York, N.Y. 10022